Color Test Page

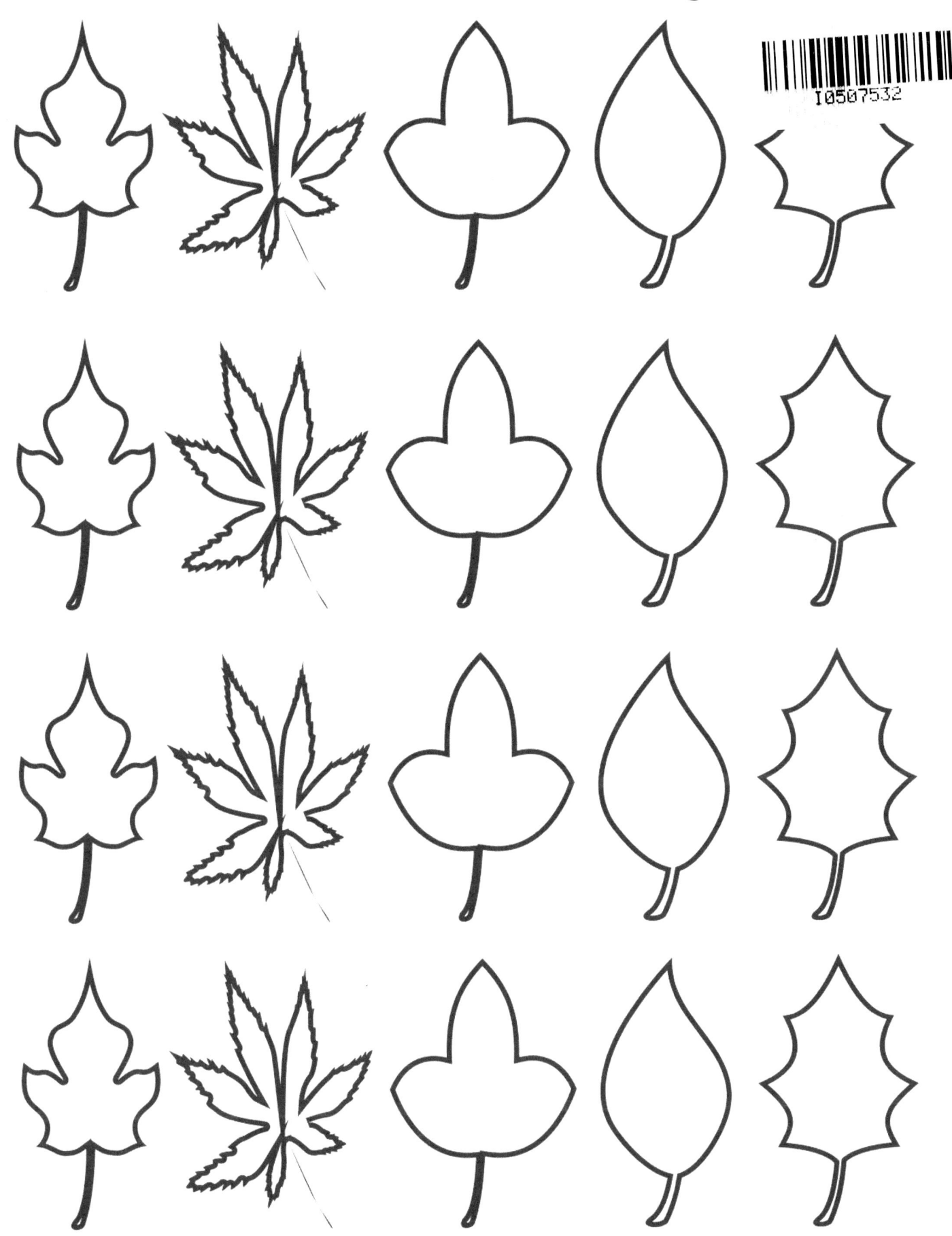

Adult Coloring Book for Relaxation Landscapes by CS Krstich

The Cross Little Institute of Relaxation Therapy

Copyright © 2018 The Cross Little Company

All rights reserved.

ISBN: 9781731112422
Imprint: Independently published

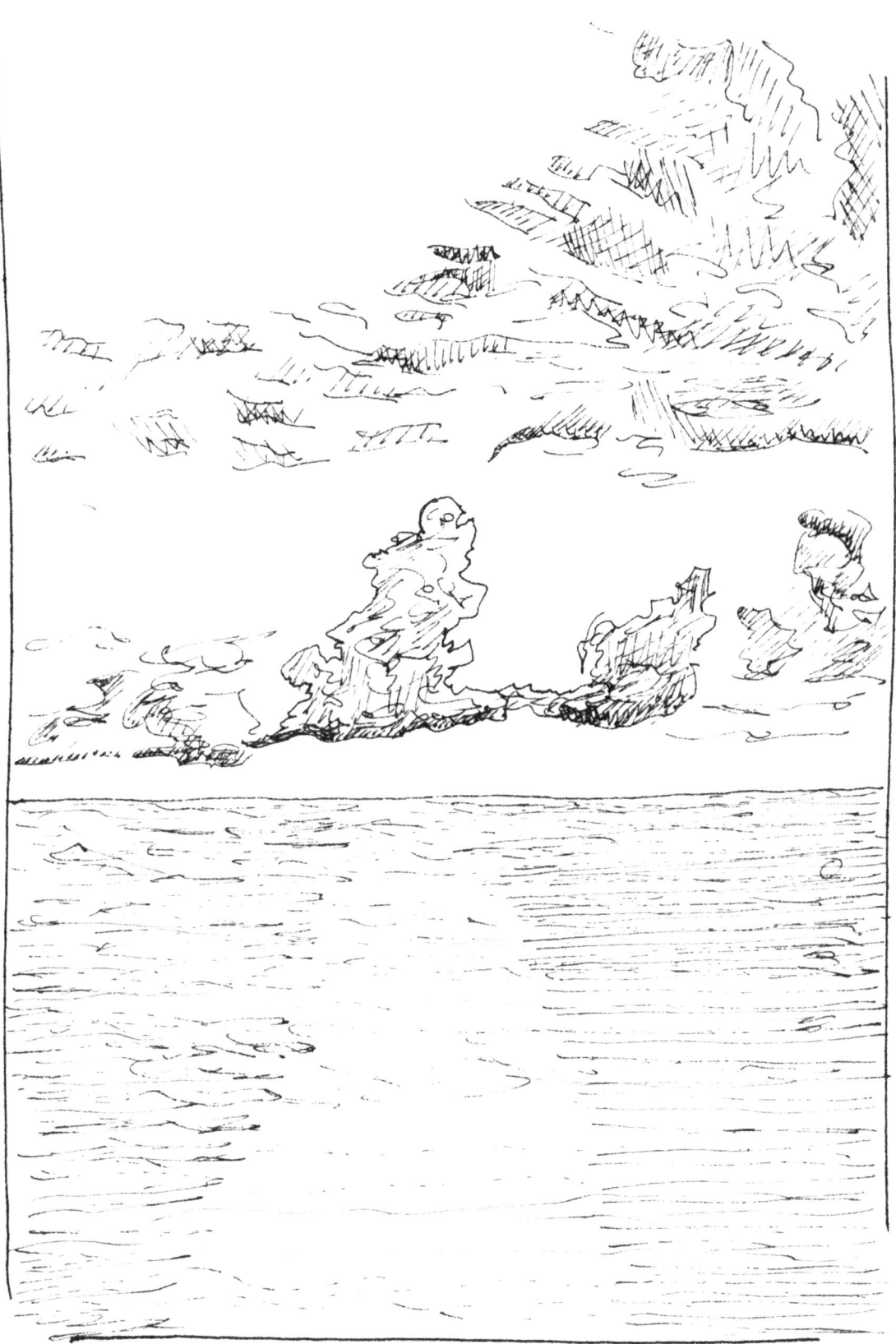

Ocean Clouds   Jan 01, '01   CRK

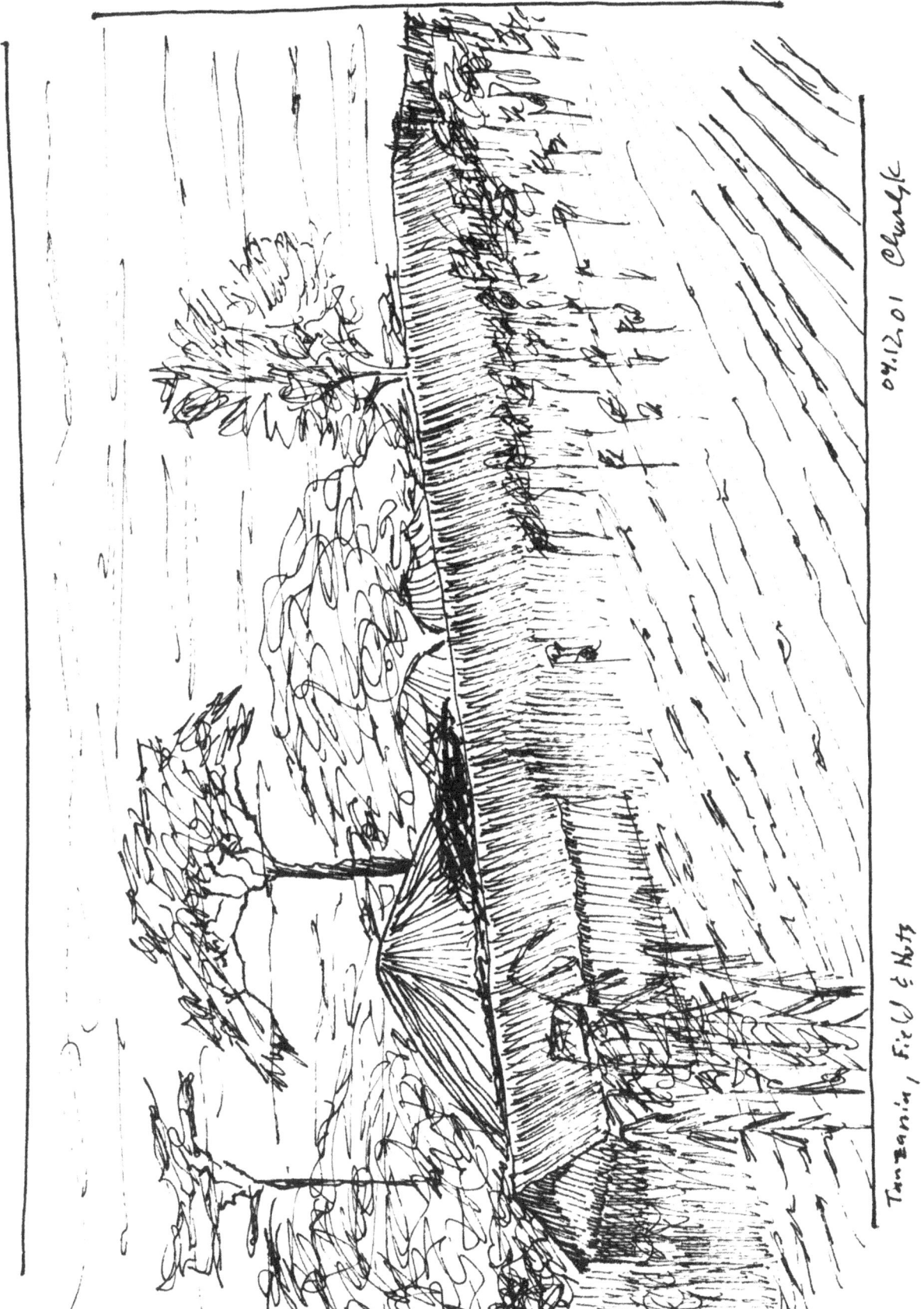

"Wampum Lake, Southwest Point" 09.13.01 @ChuckK

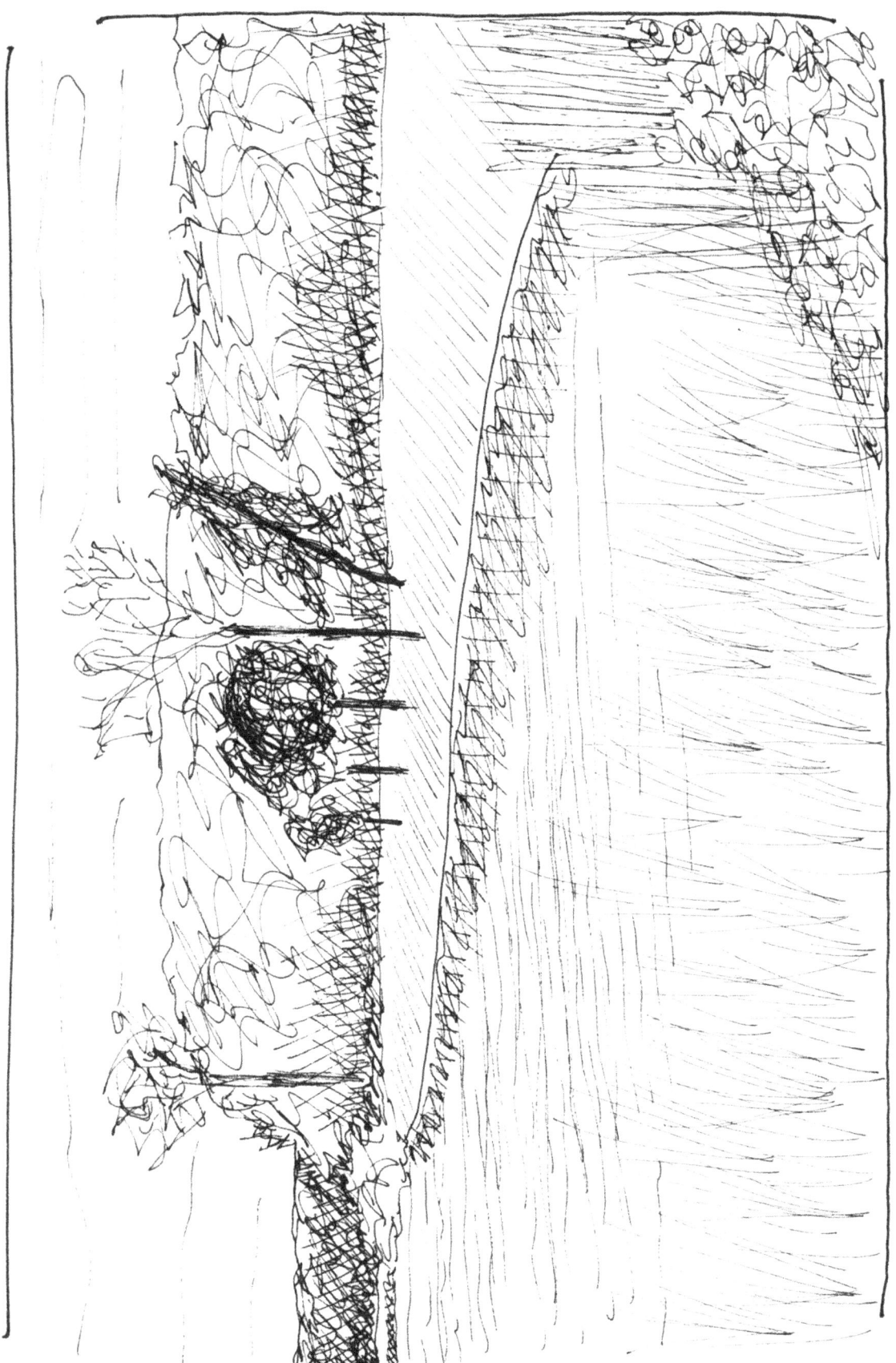

"Wampum Lake, South Point with Weeds" 08.14.01 Chung/c

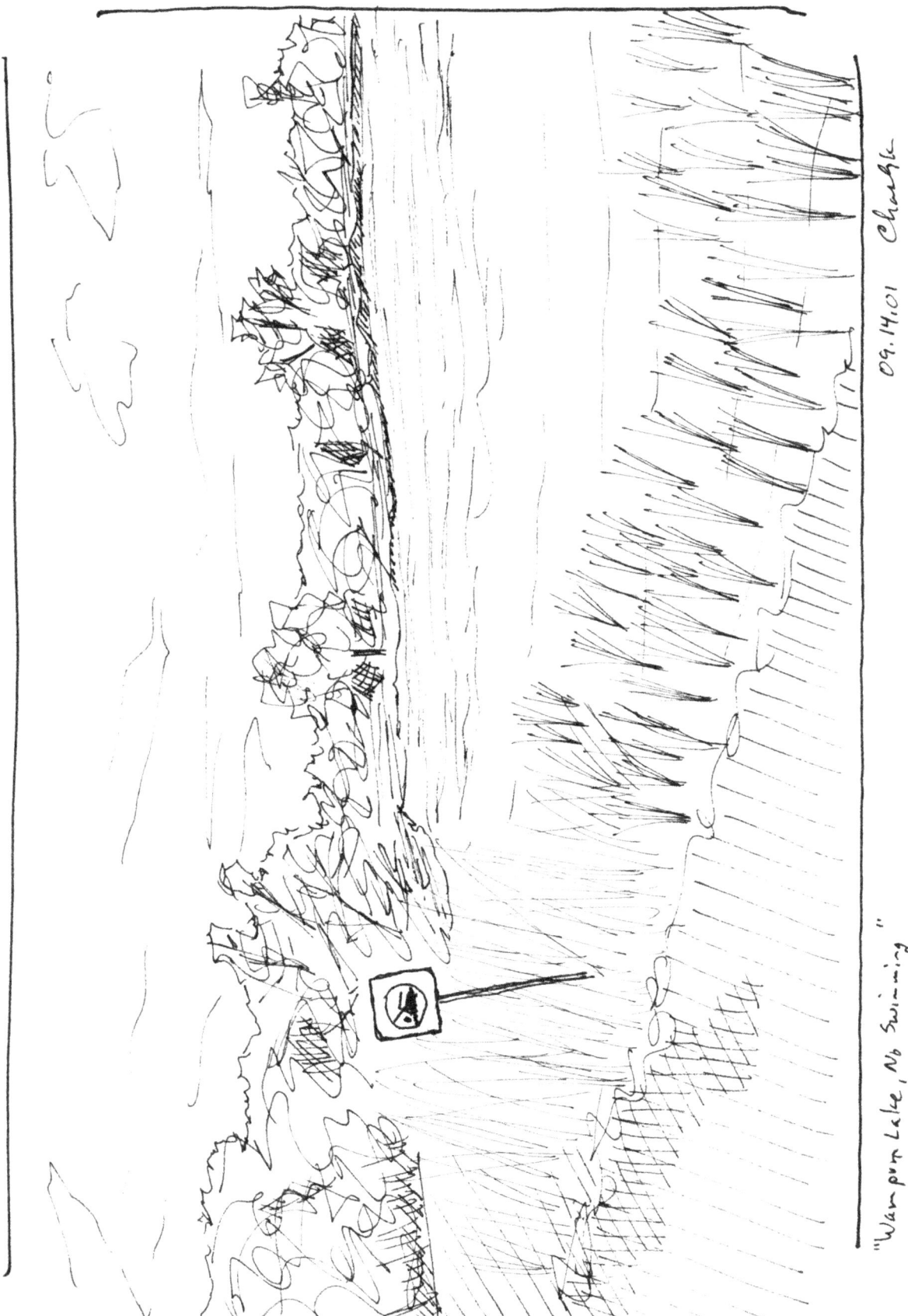

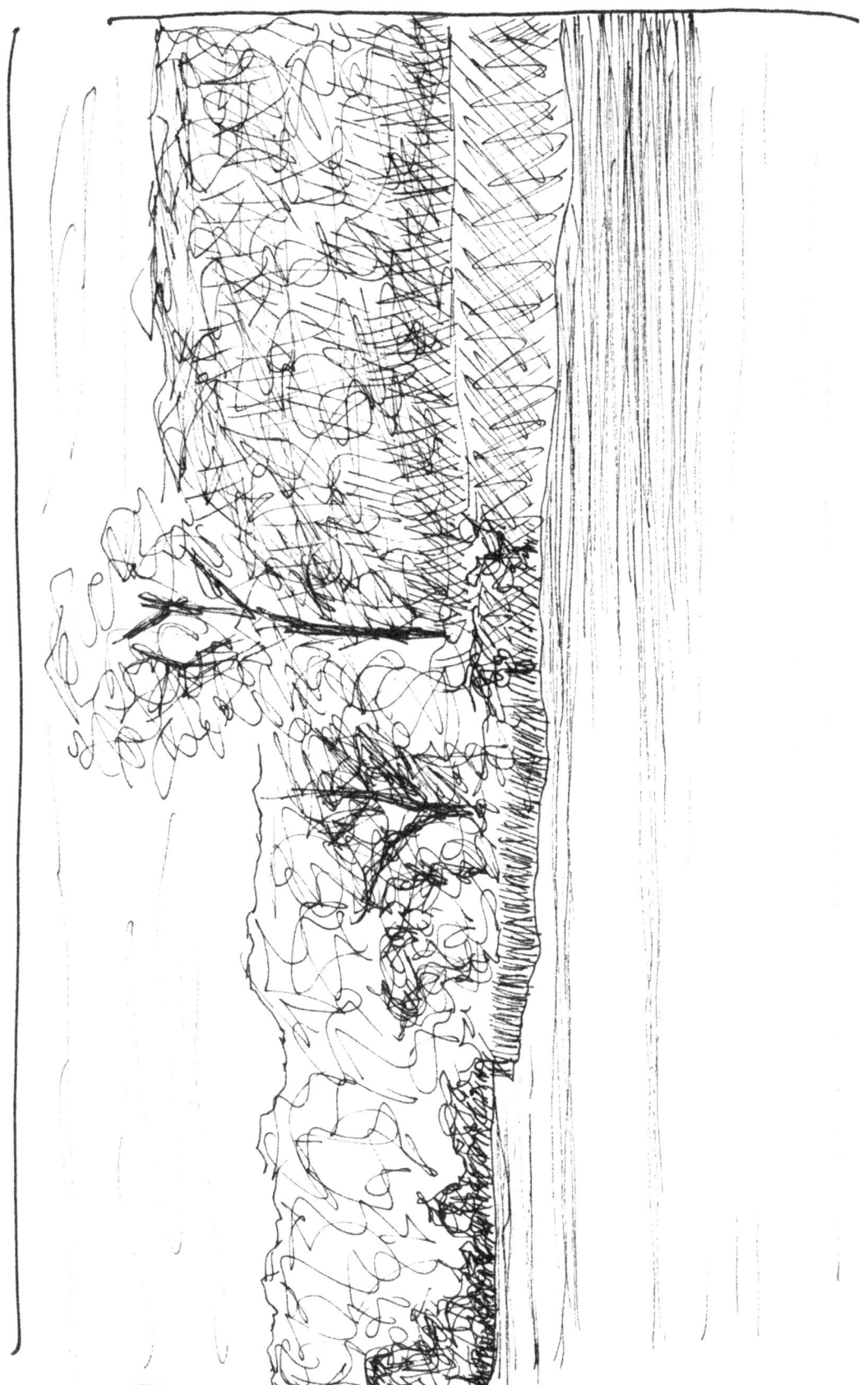

"Wampum Lake, South Bank" 09.16.01

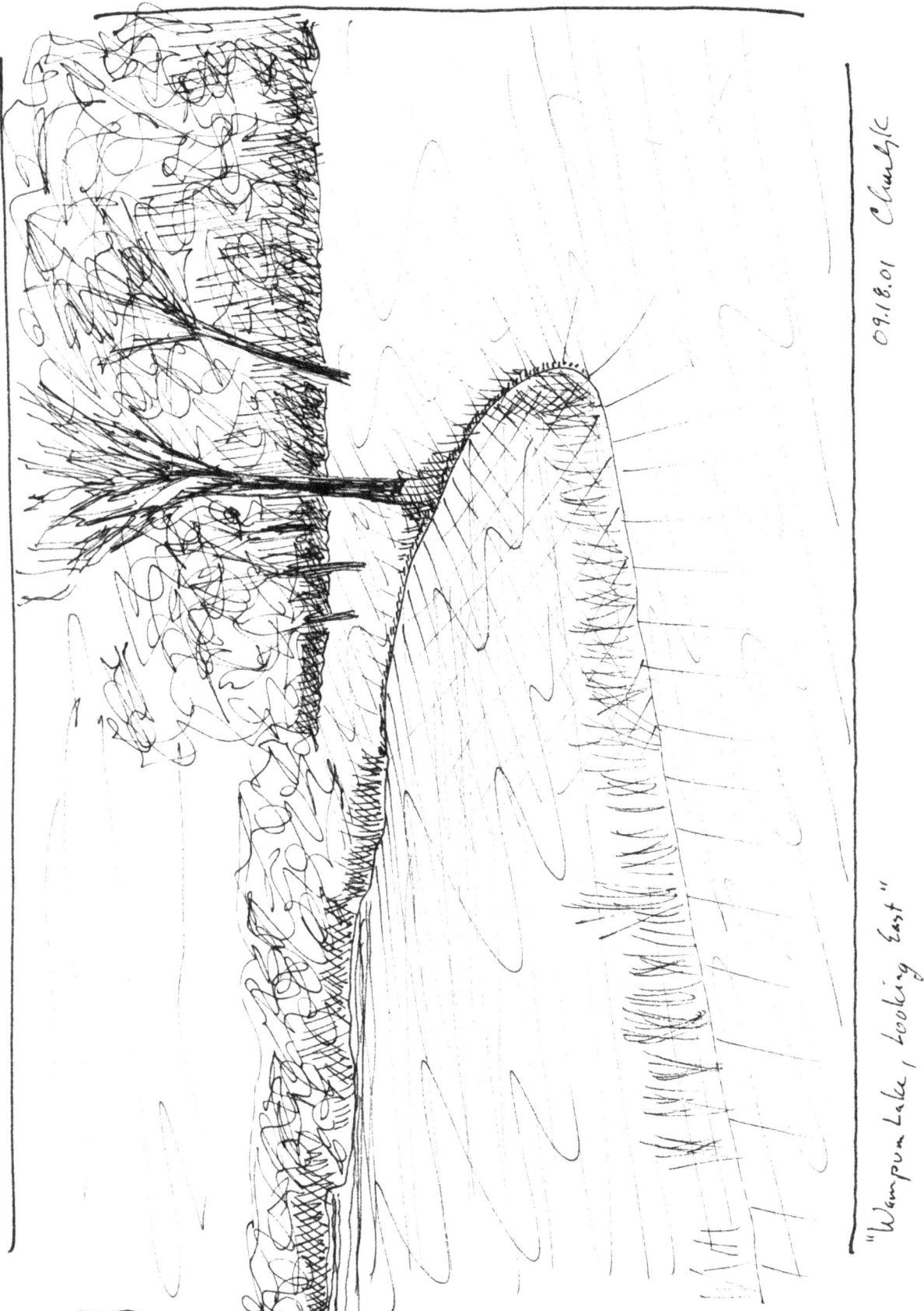

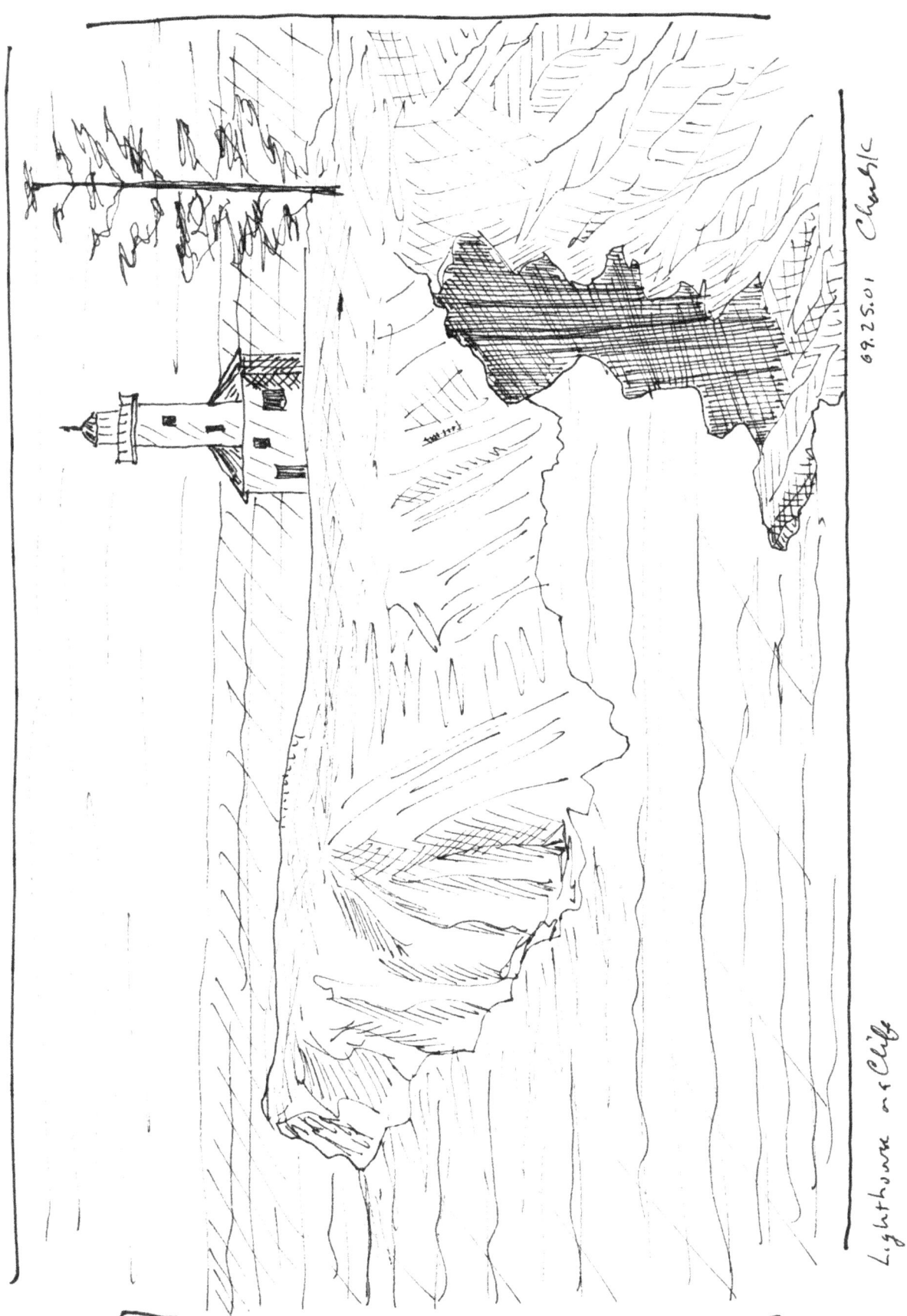

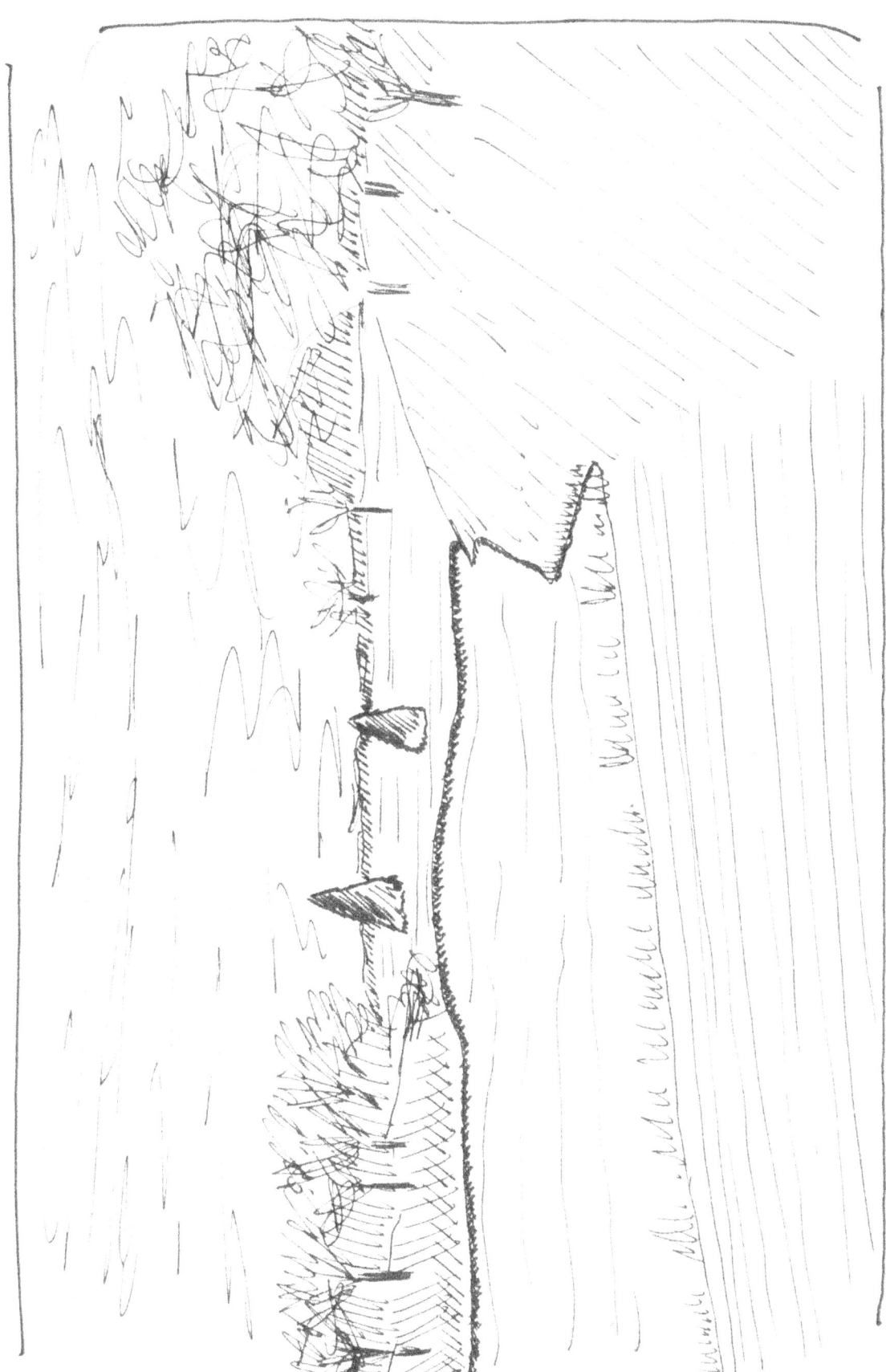

"Biology Pond, North Point" 02.22.02 Church

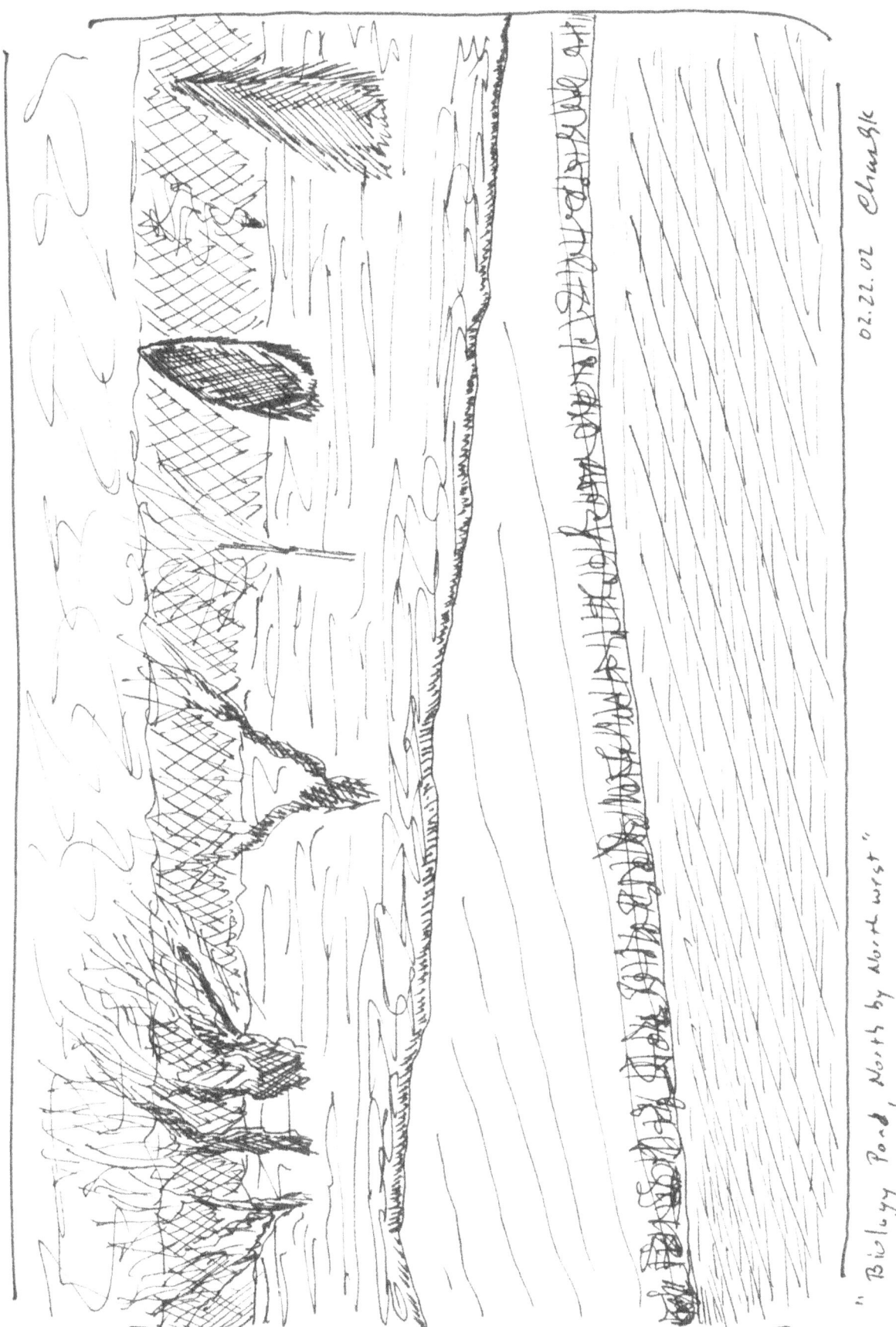

"Biology Pond, North by Northwest" 02.22.02

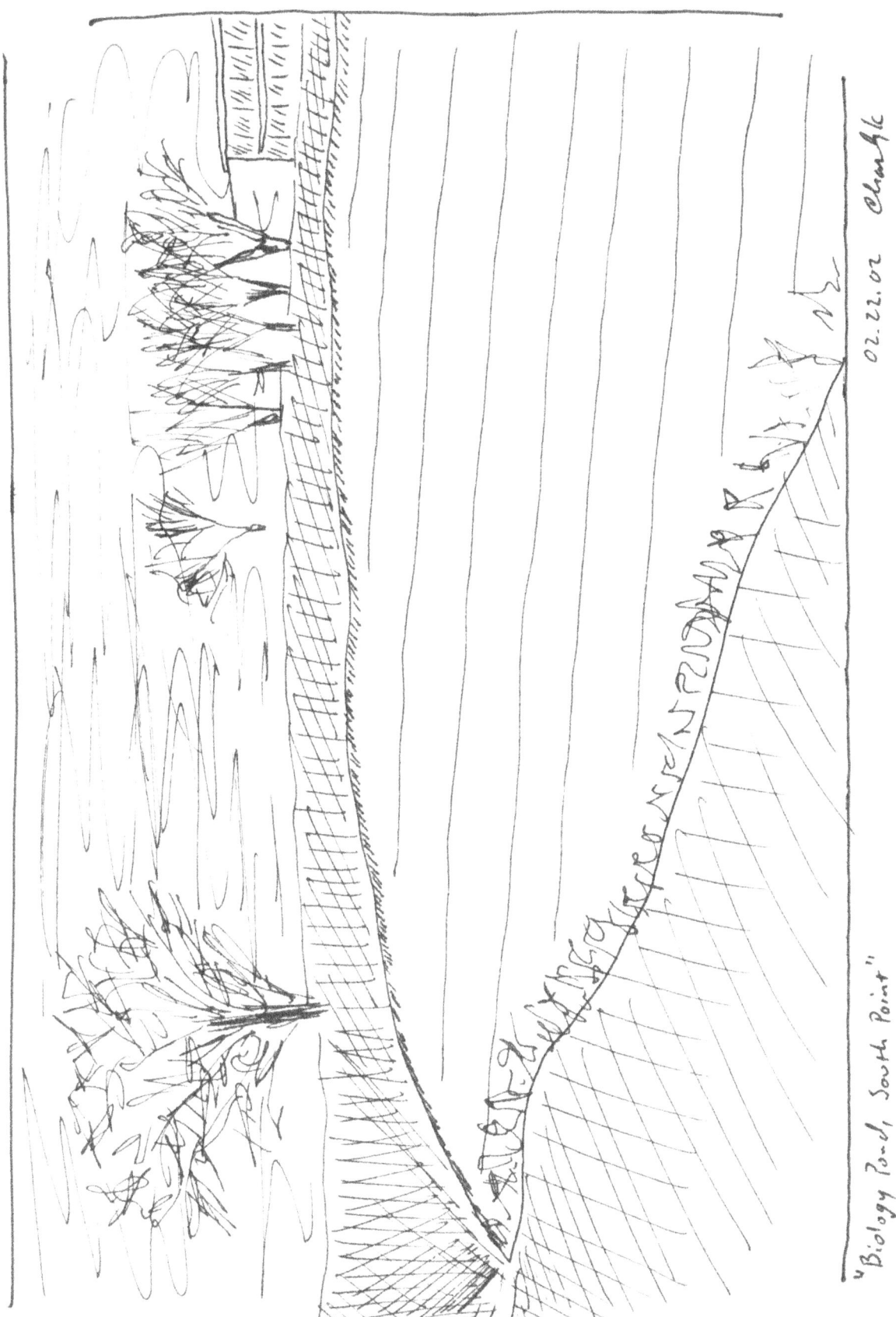

"Biology Pond, South Point" 02.22.02 @lmAk

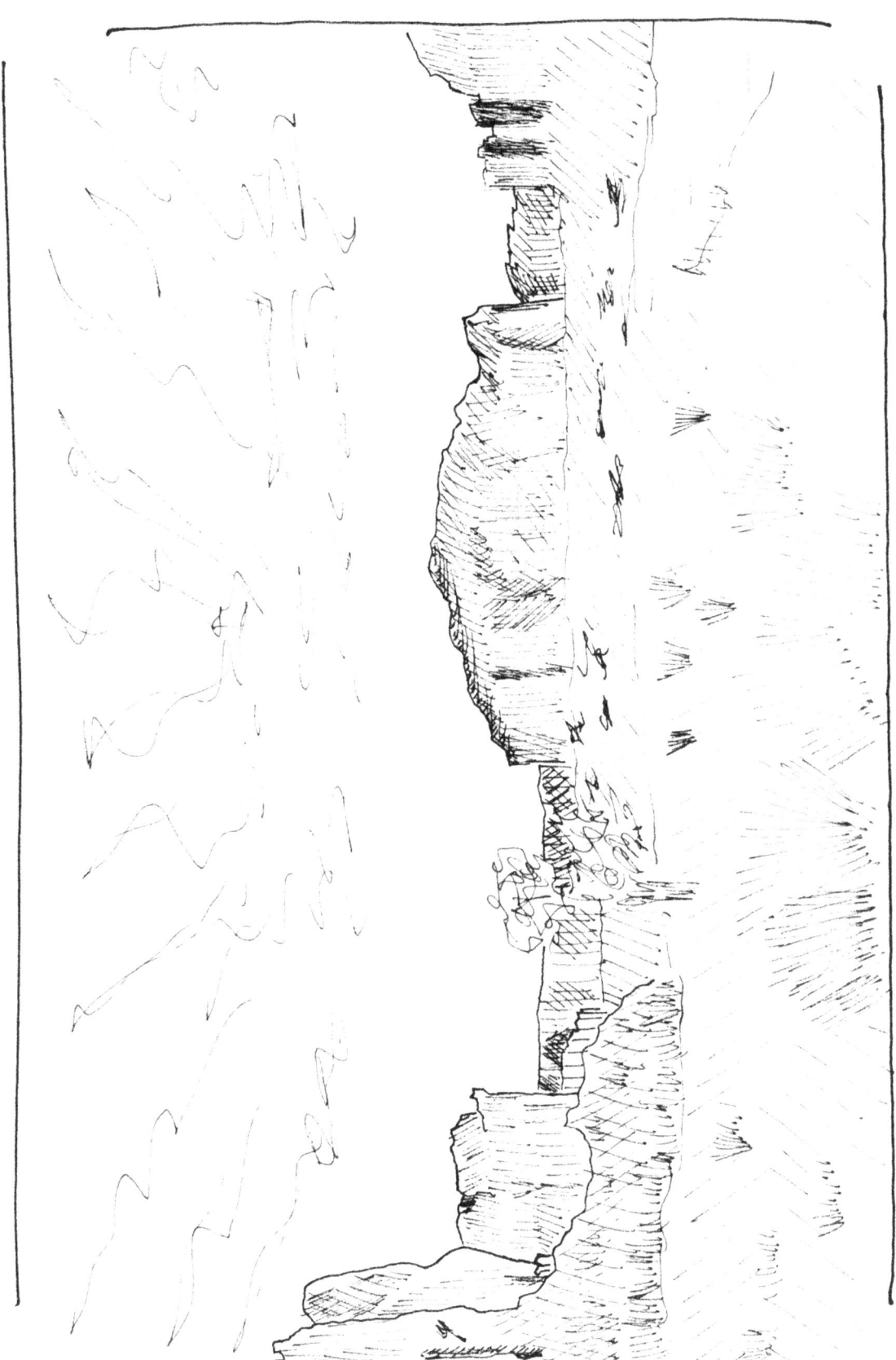

Desert, Monument Valley with clouds 03.27.01 Chuck

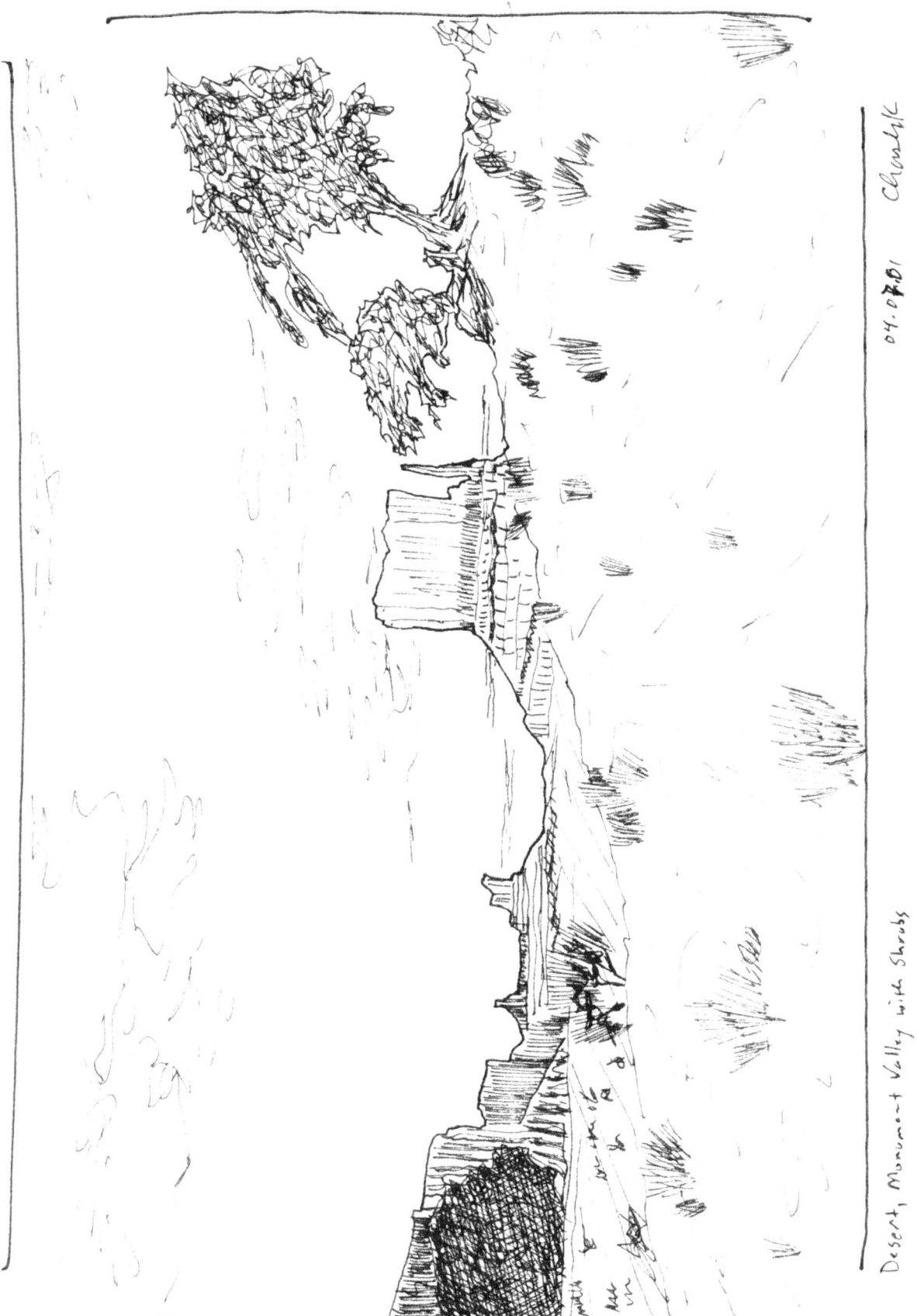

Desert, Monument Valley with Shrubs — 04.07.01 Charlik

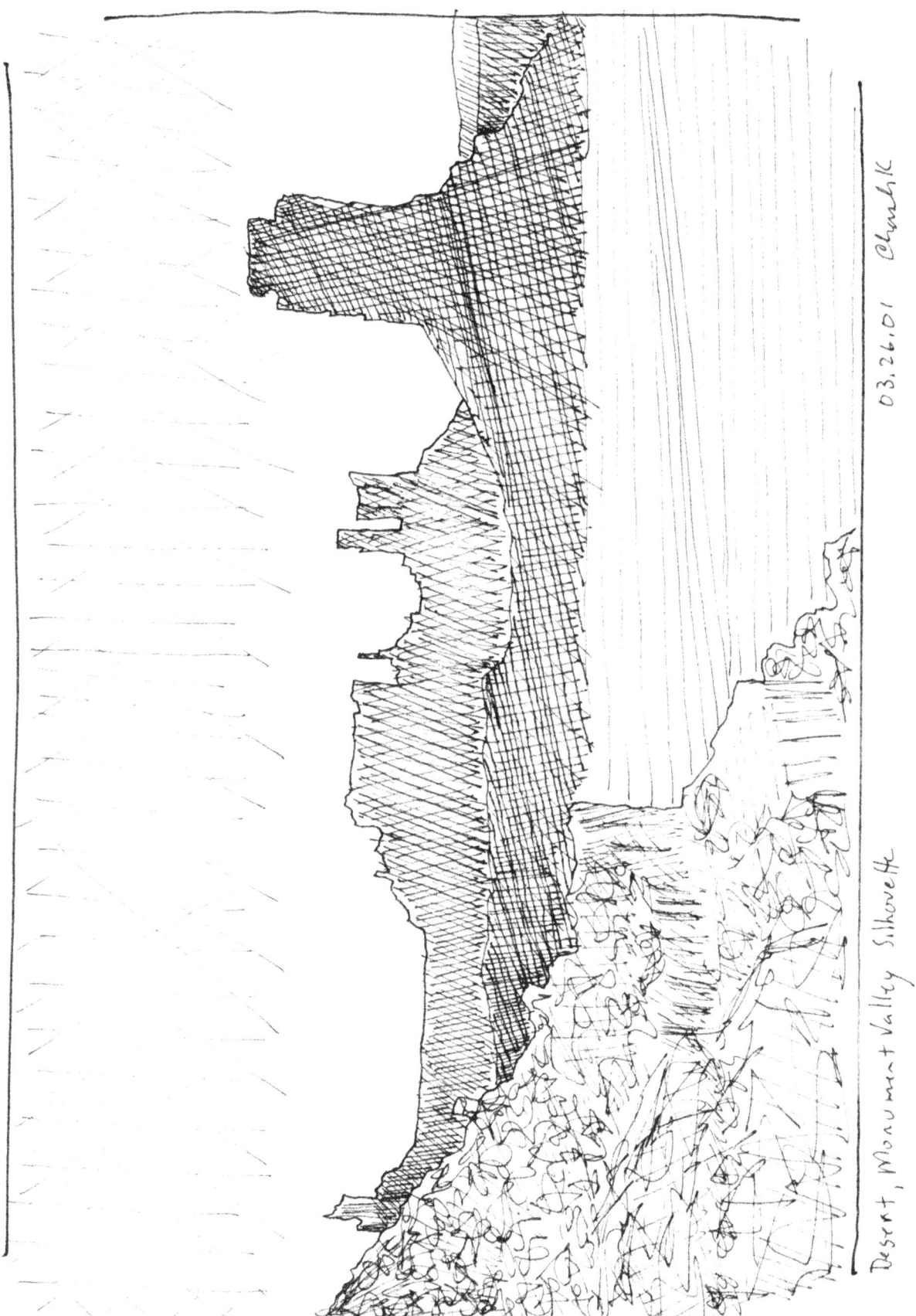

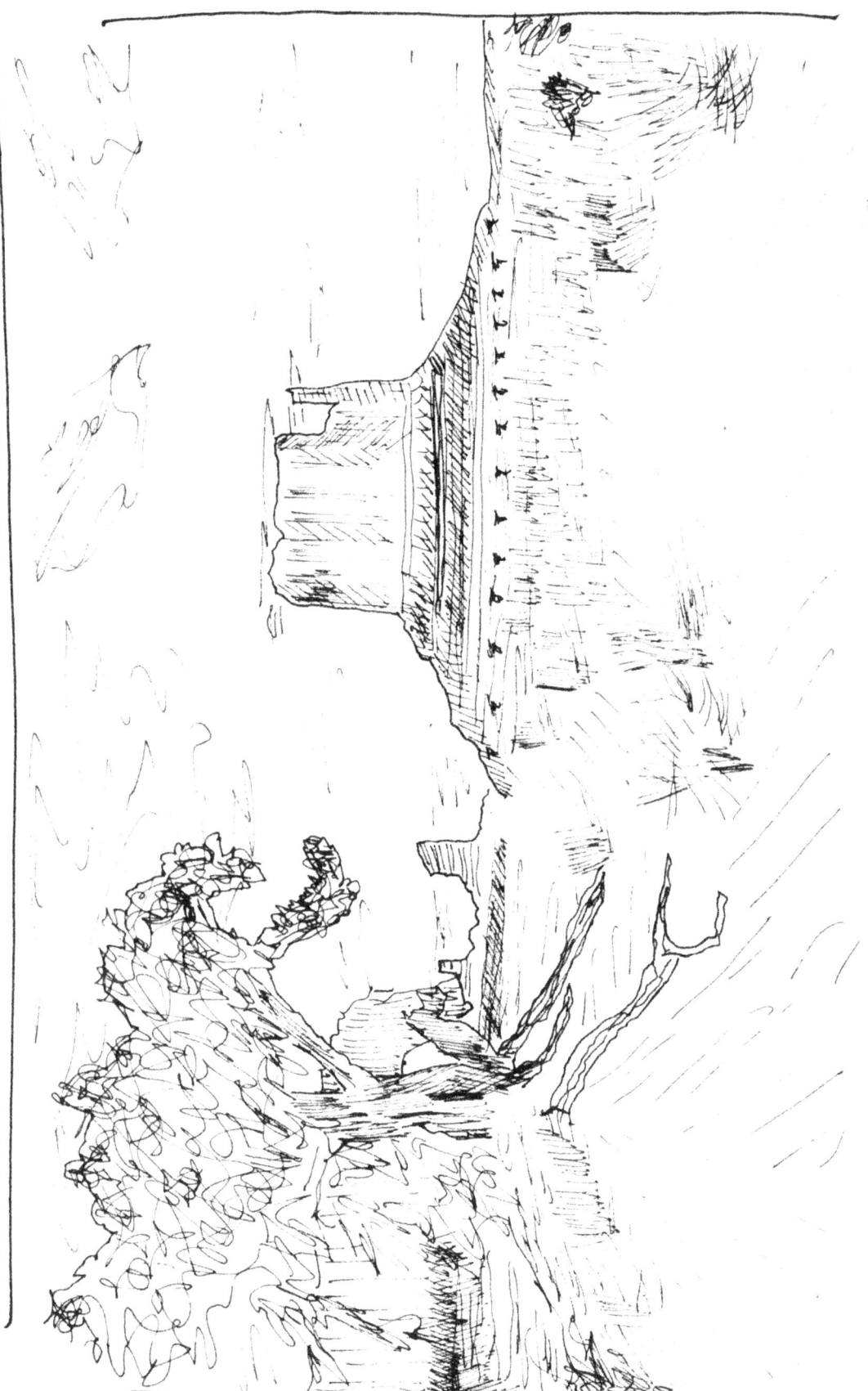

Desert, Monument Valley with Tree 04.02.01 Cheatle

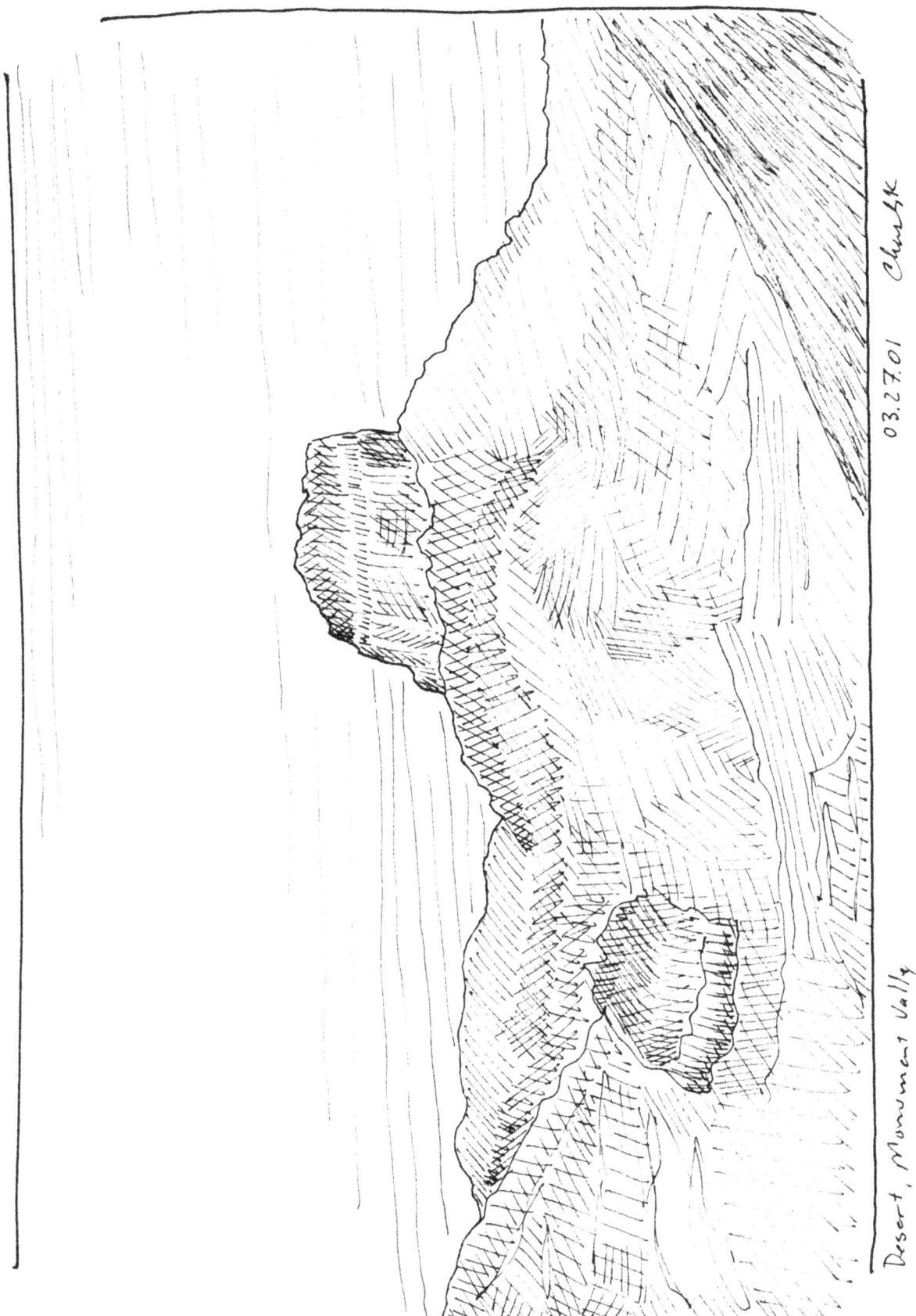

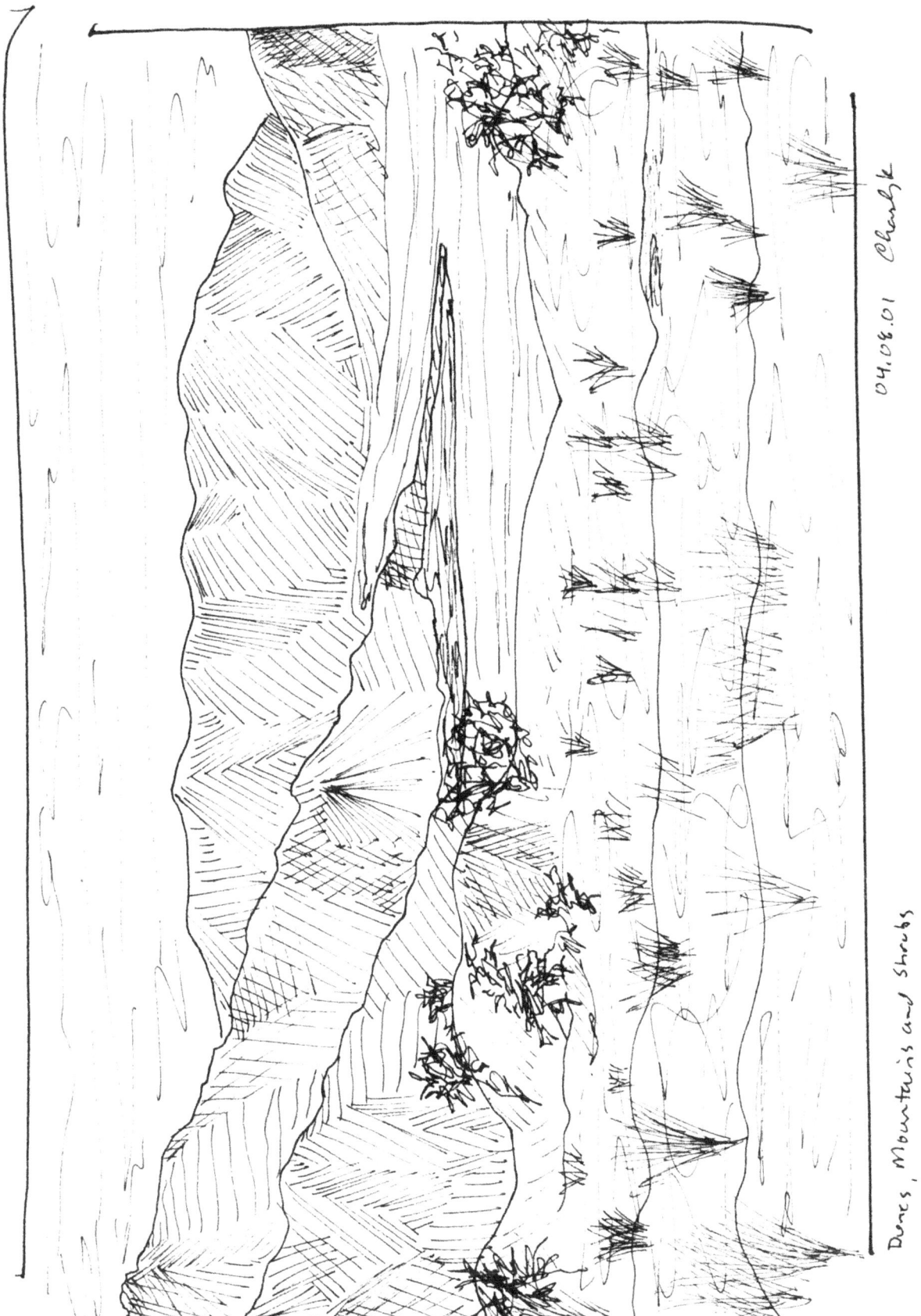

Dunes, Mountains and Shrubs — 04.08.01 Chadyk

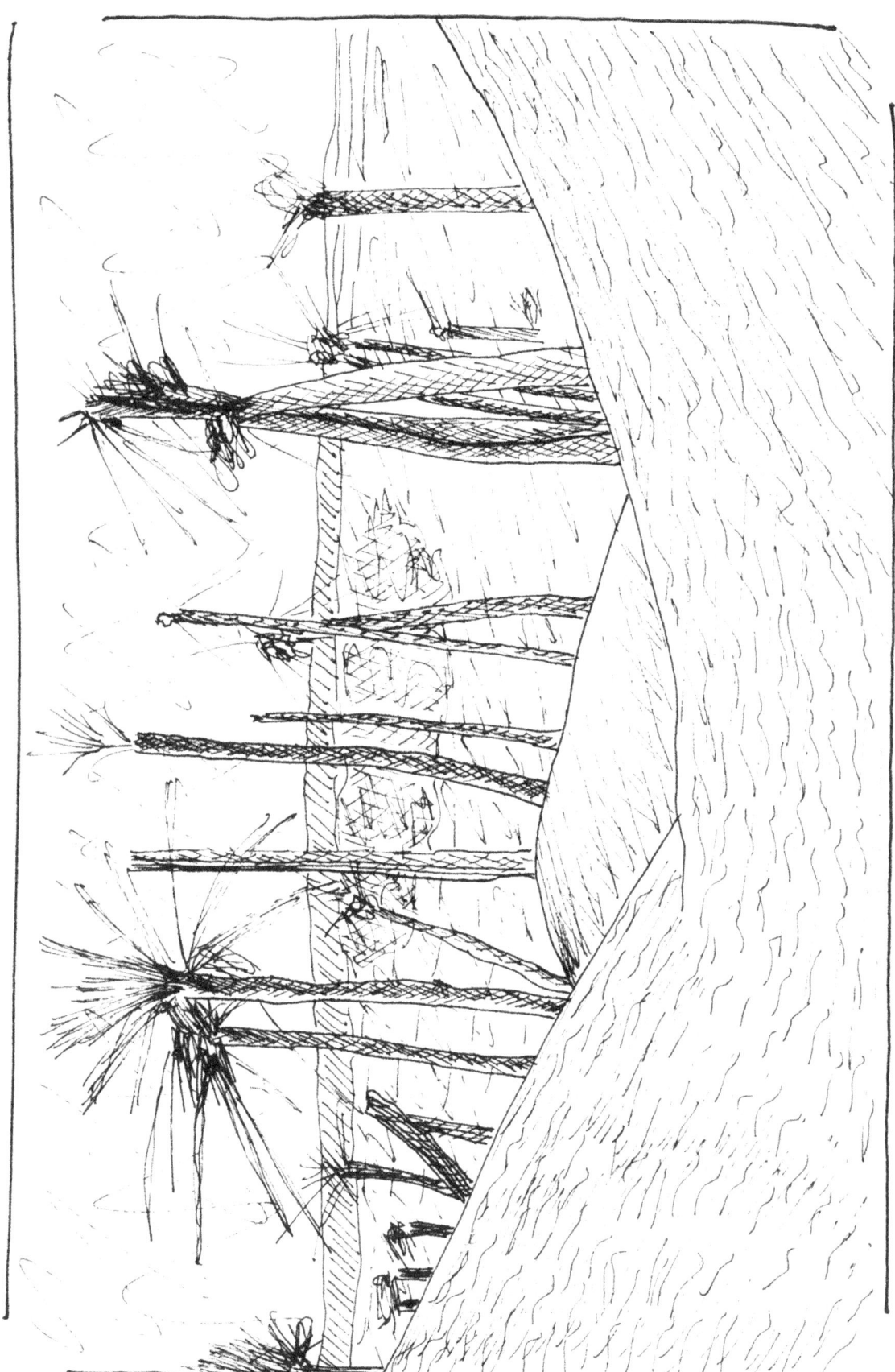

Dunes After A Storm　04.09.01 Chundyk

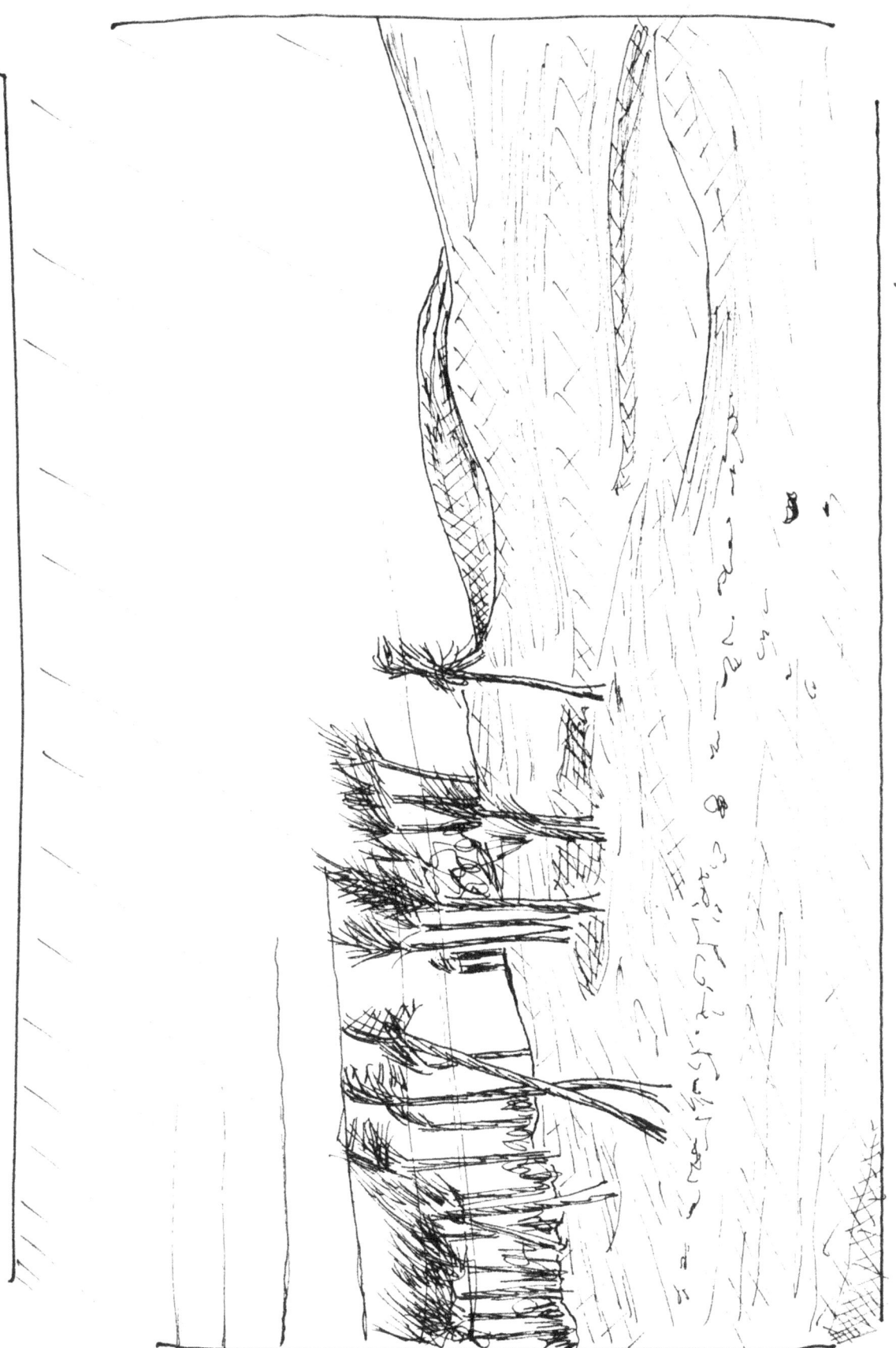

Dunes, Wind Blown Palms — 04.08.01 Chuck

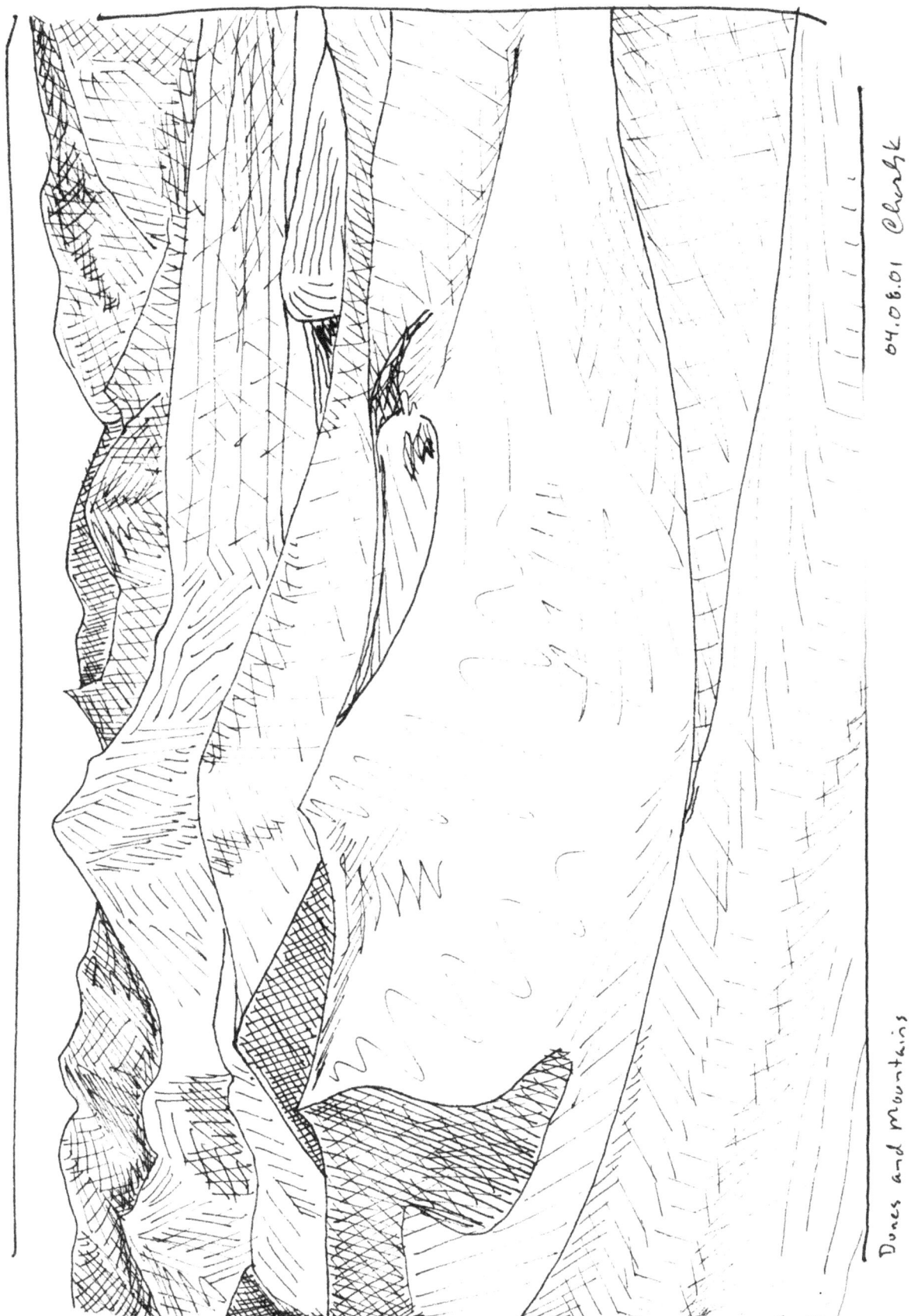

Dunes and Mountains 04.06.01 Chushul

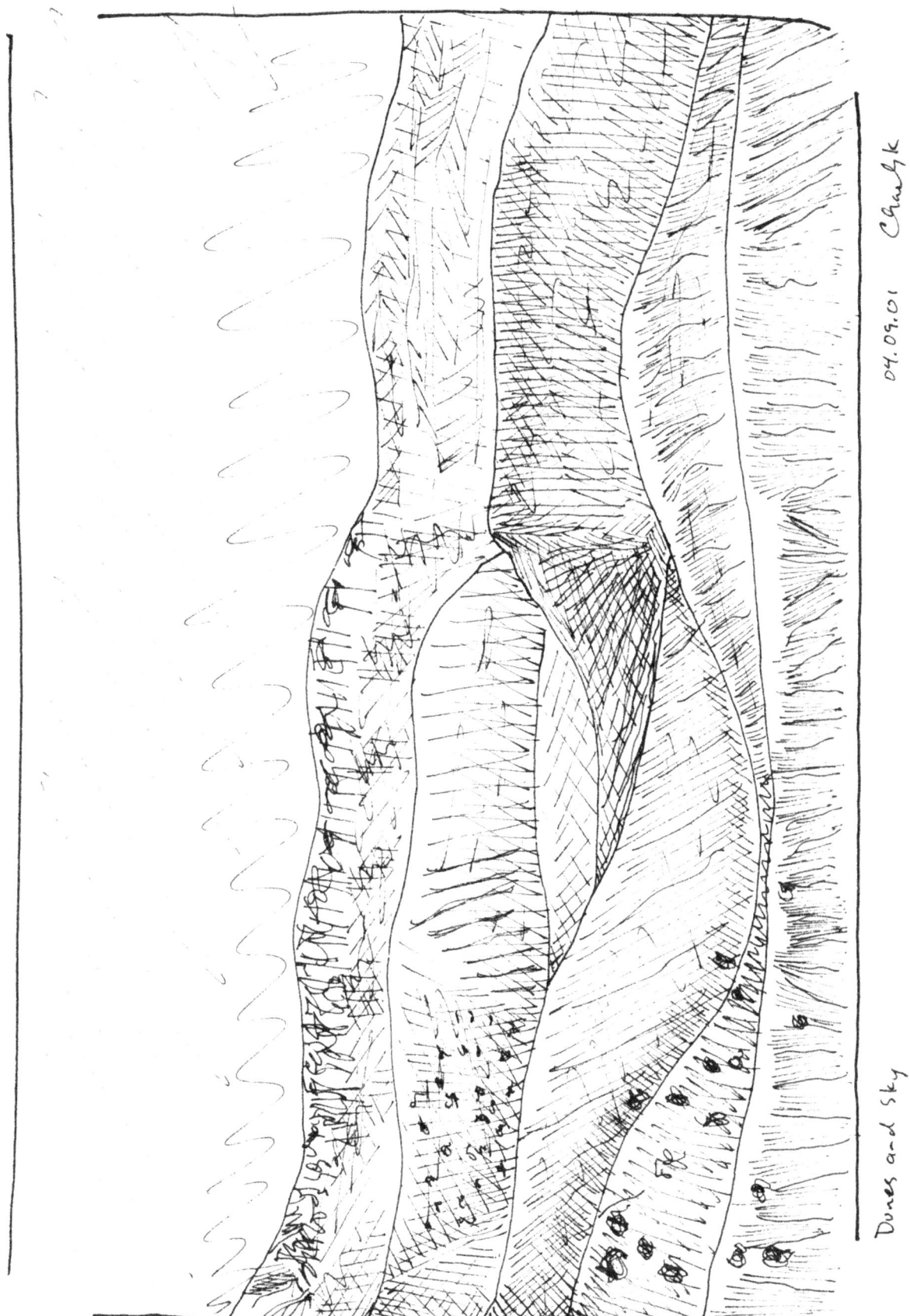

Dunes and Sky 04.09.01 Chaulk

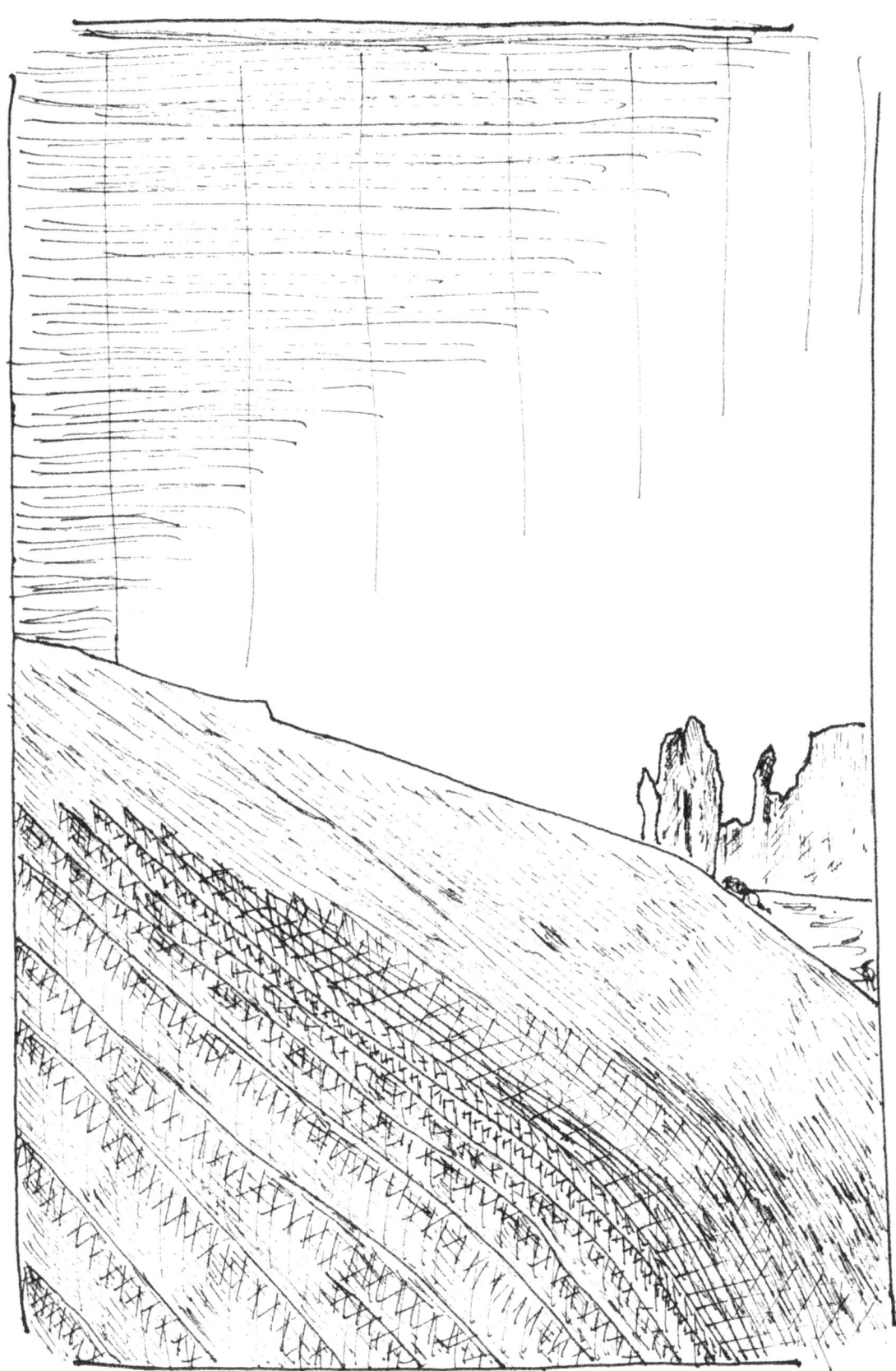

Dunes with mesa   04.10.01 Cherskyk

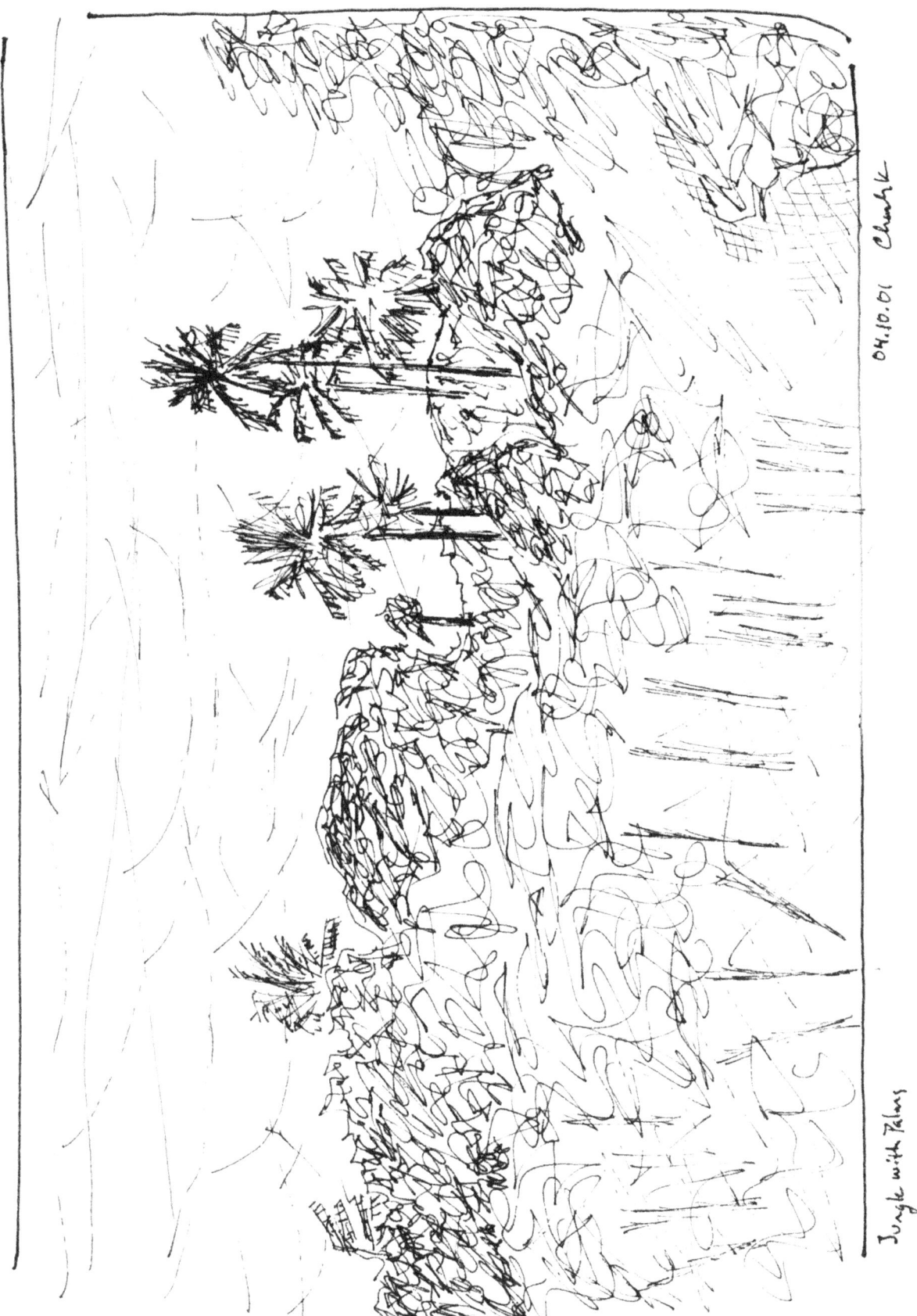

Jungle with Palms 04.10.01 Chunk

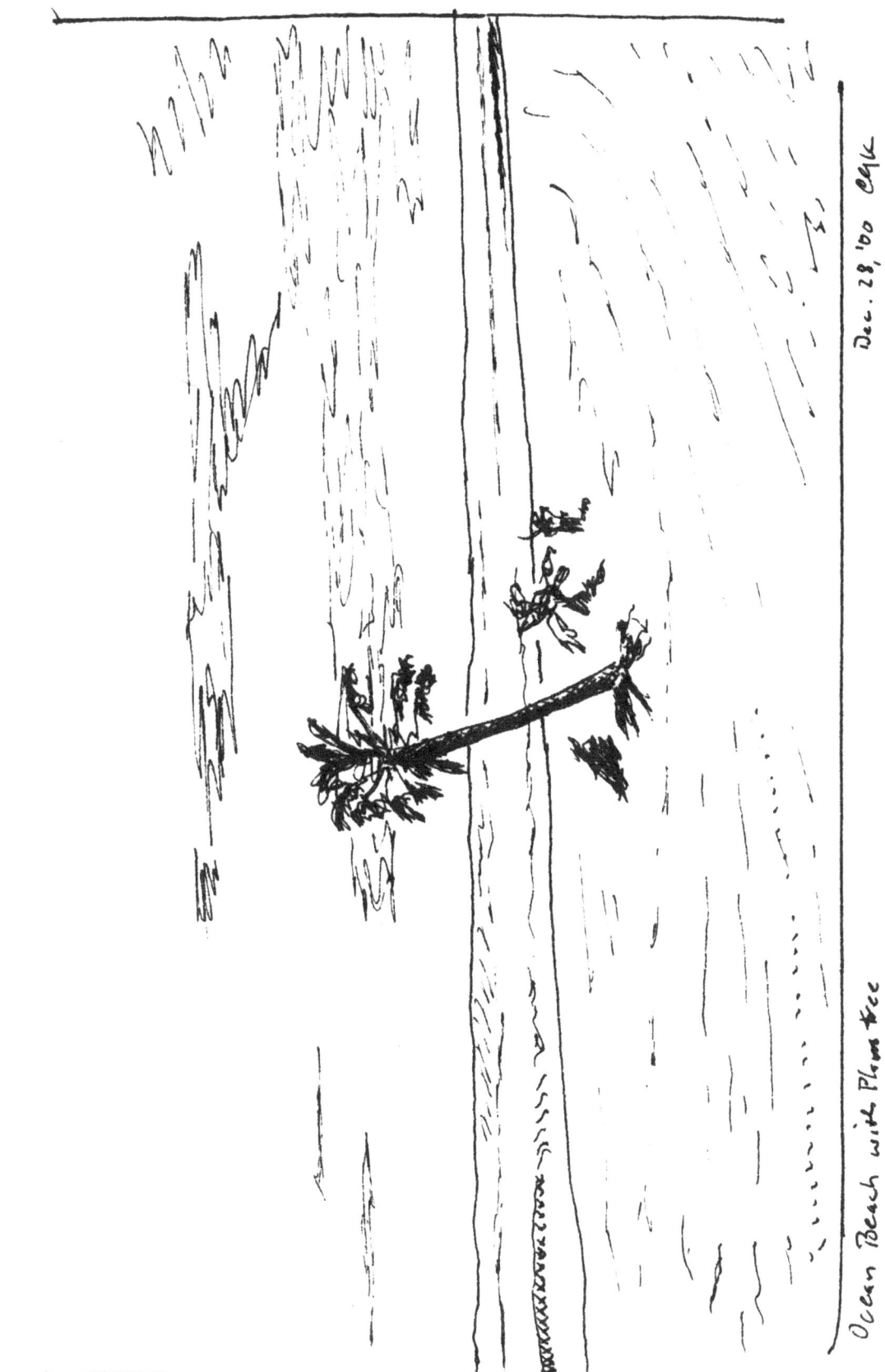

Ocean Beach with Palm tree — Dec. 28, '00 CGK

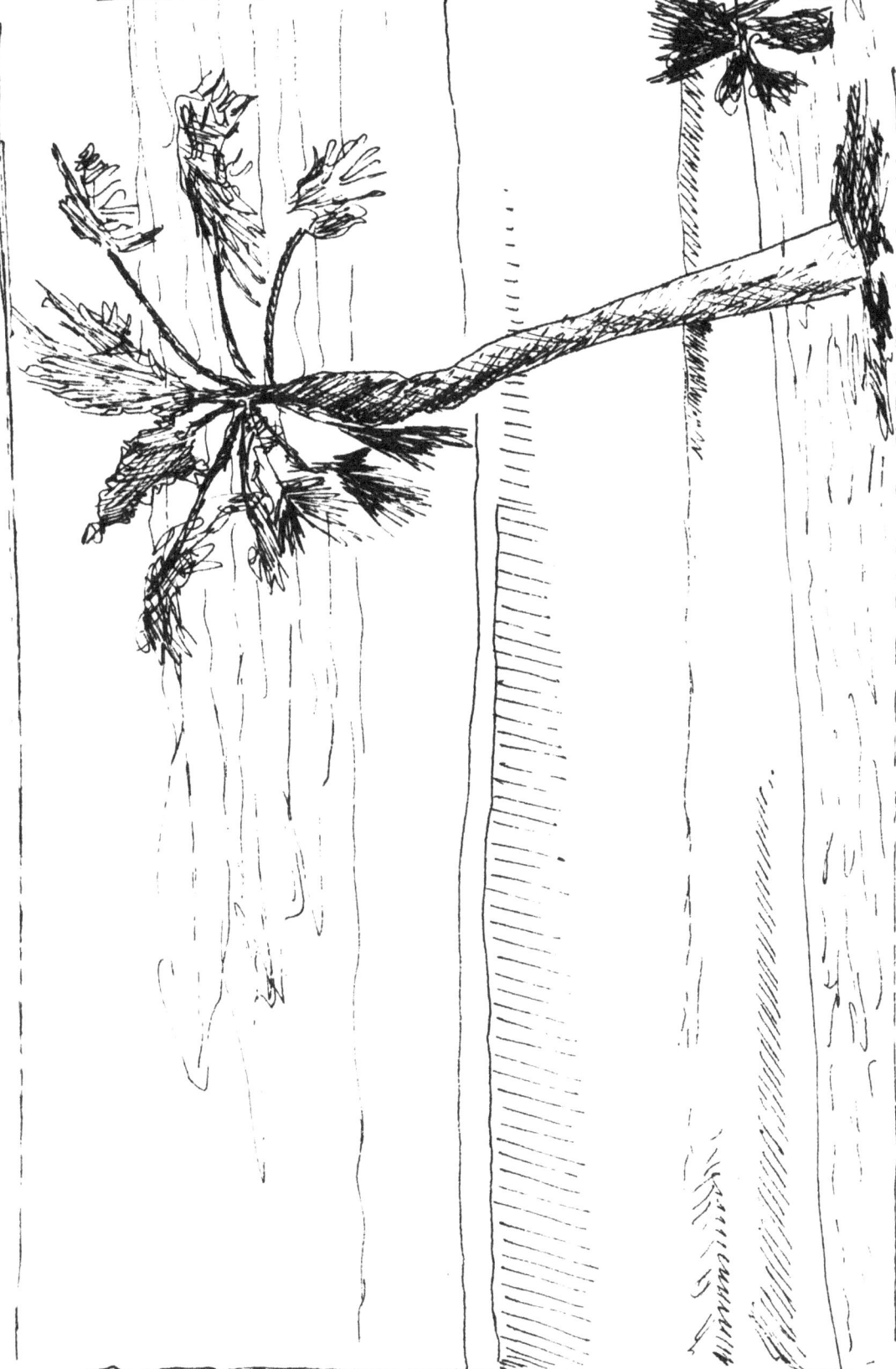

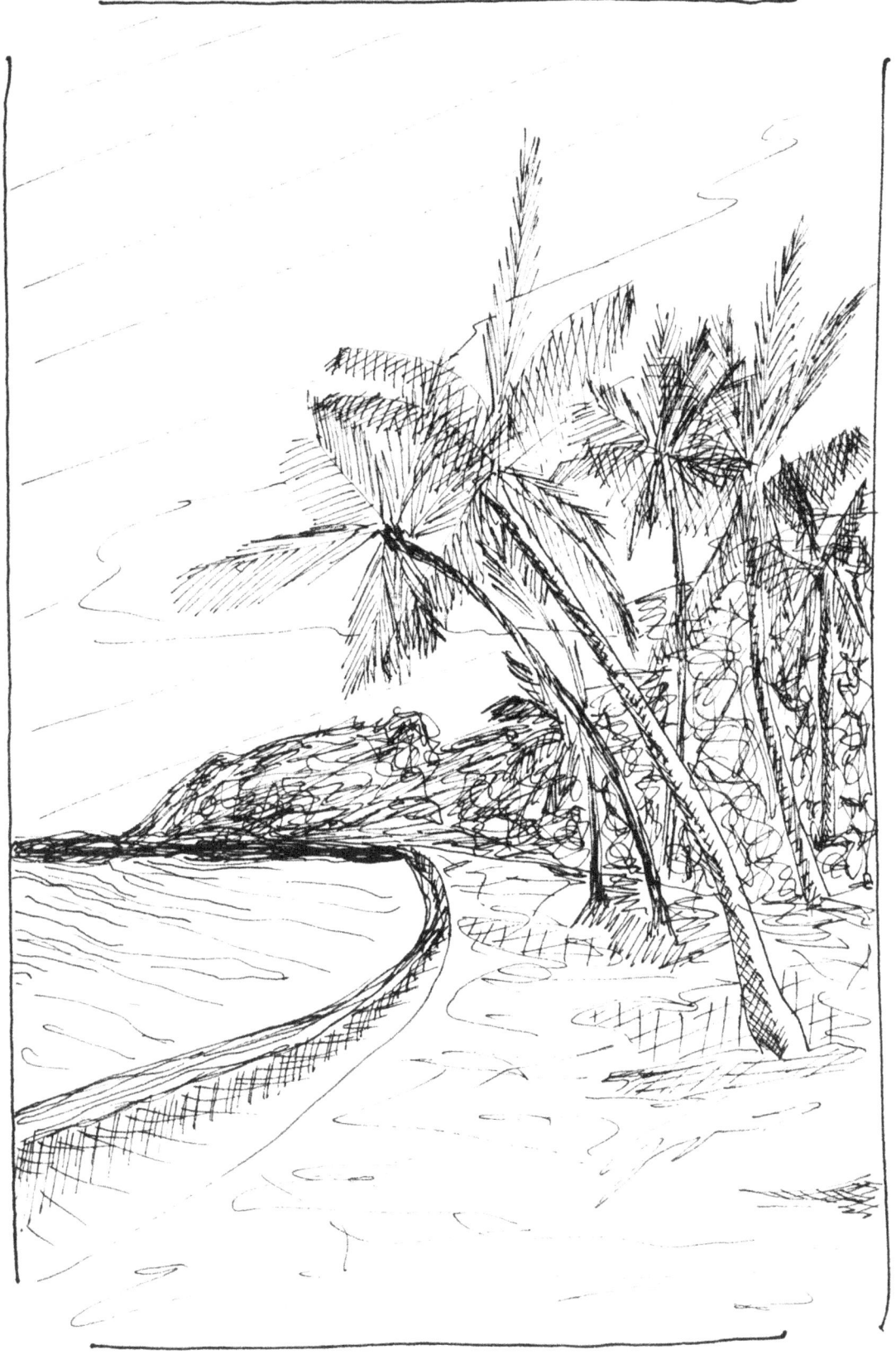

Ocean Beach, Palms 04.07.01 Cheryl K

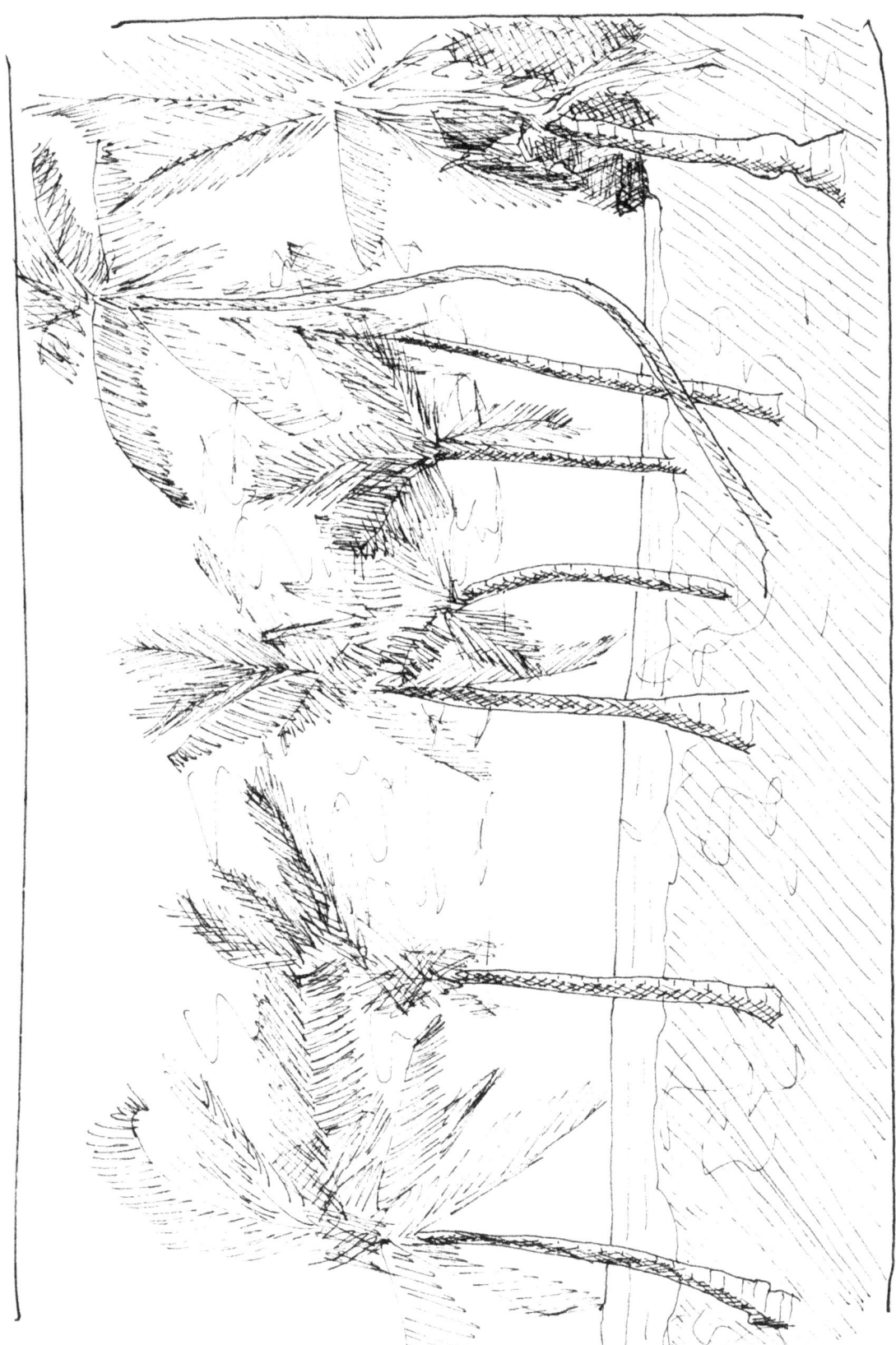

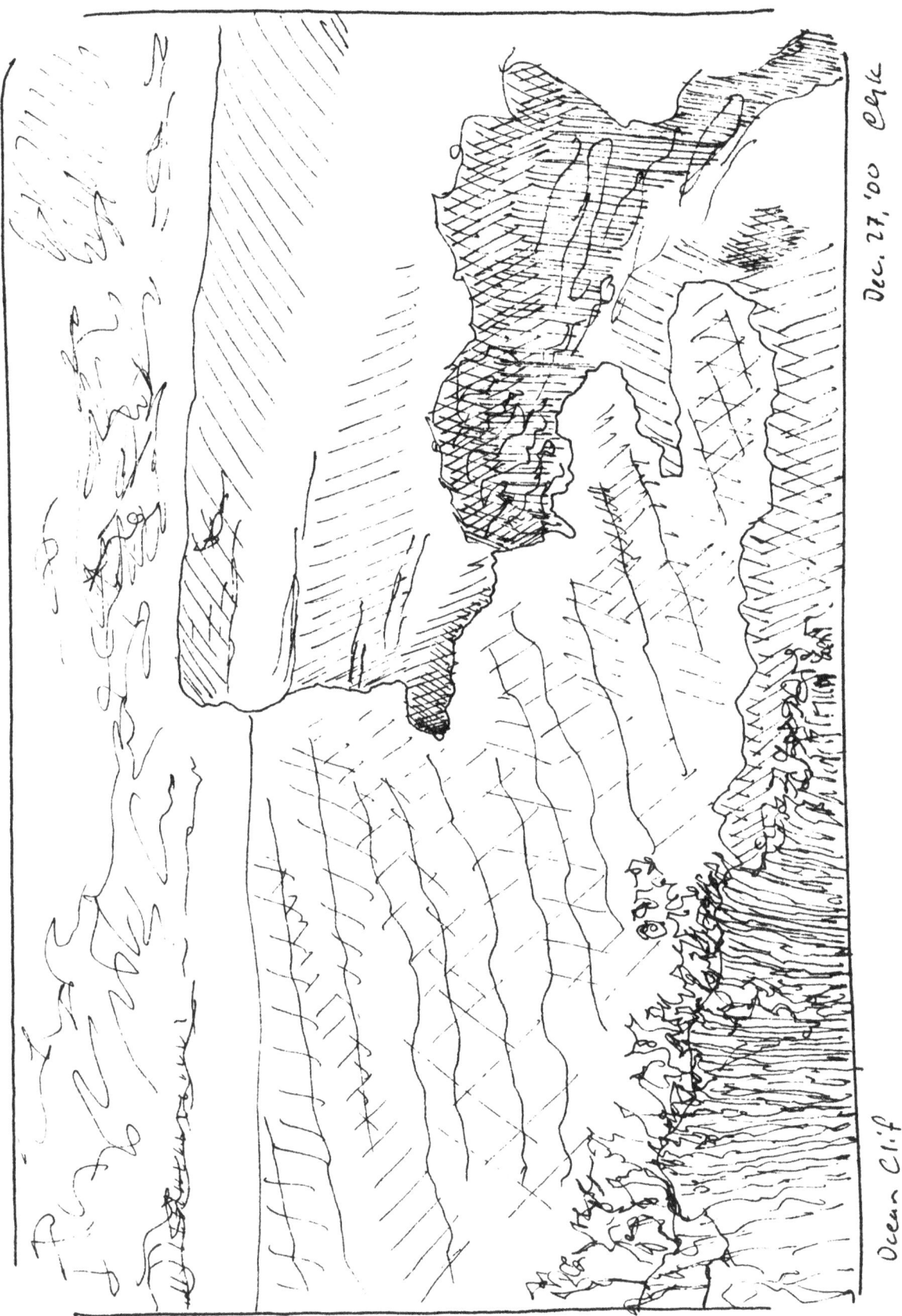

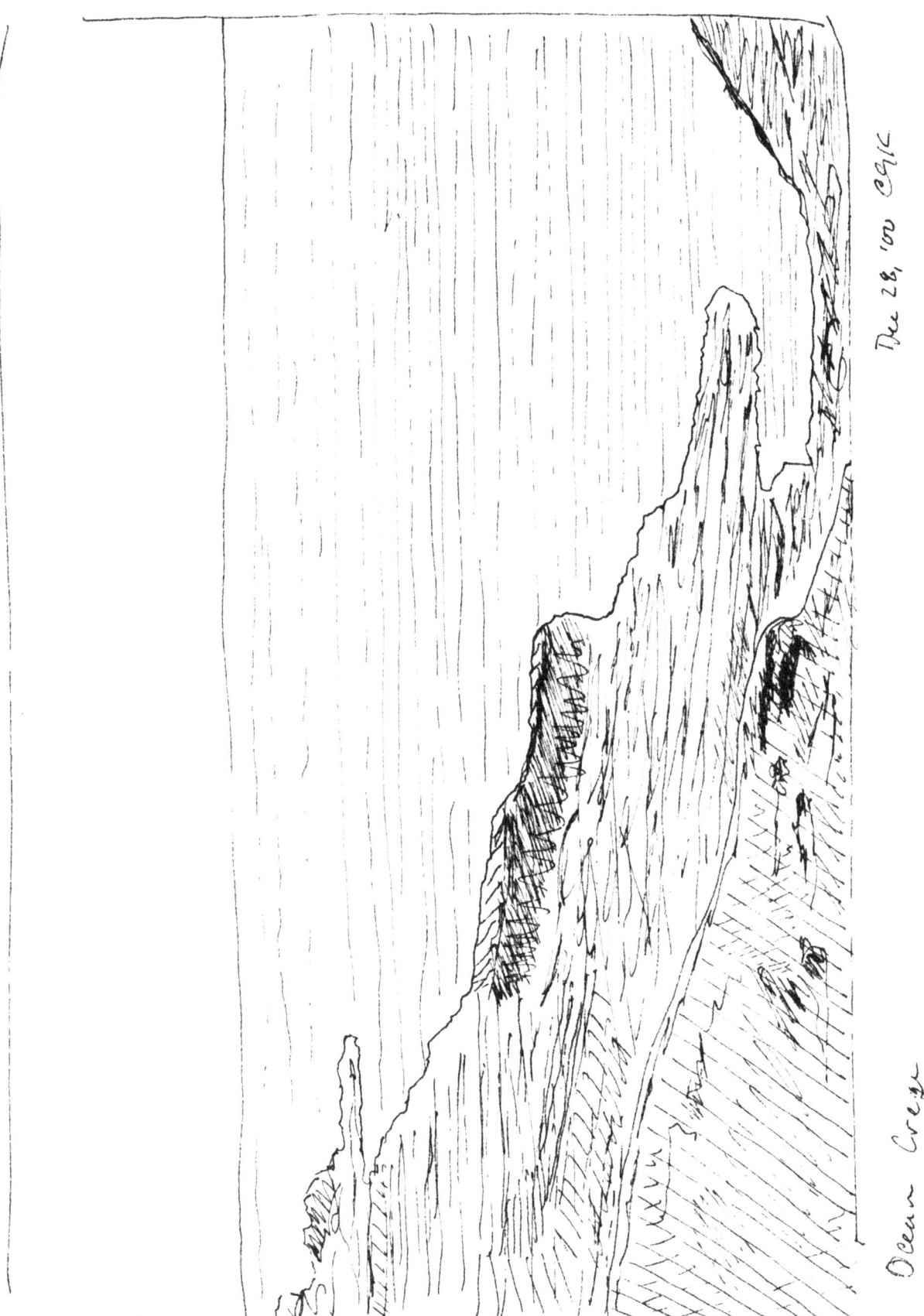

Ocean Mountain Shore   03.25.01   Montauk

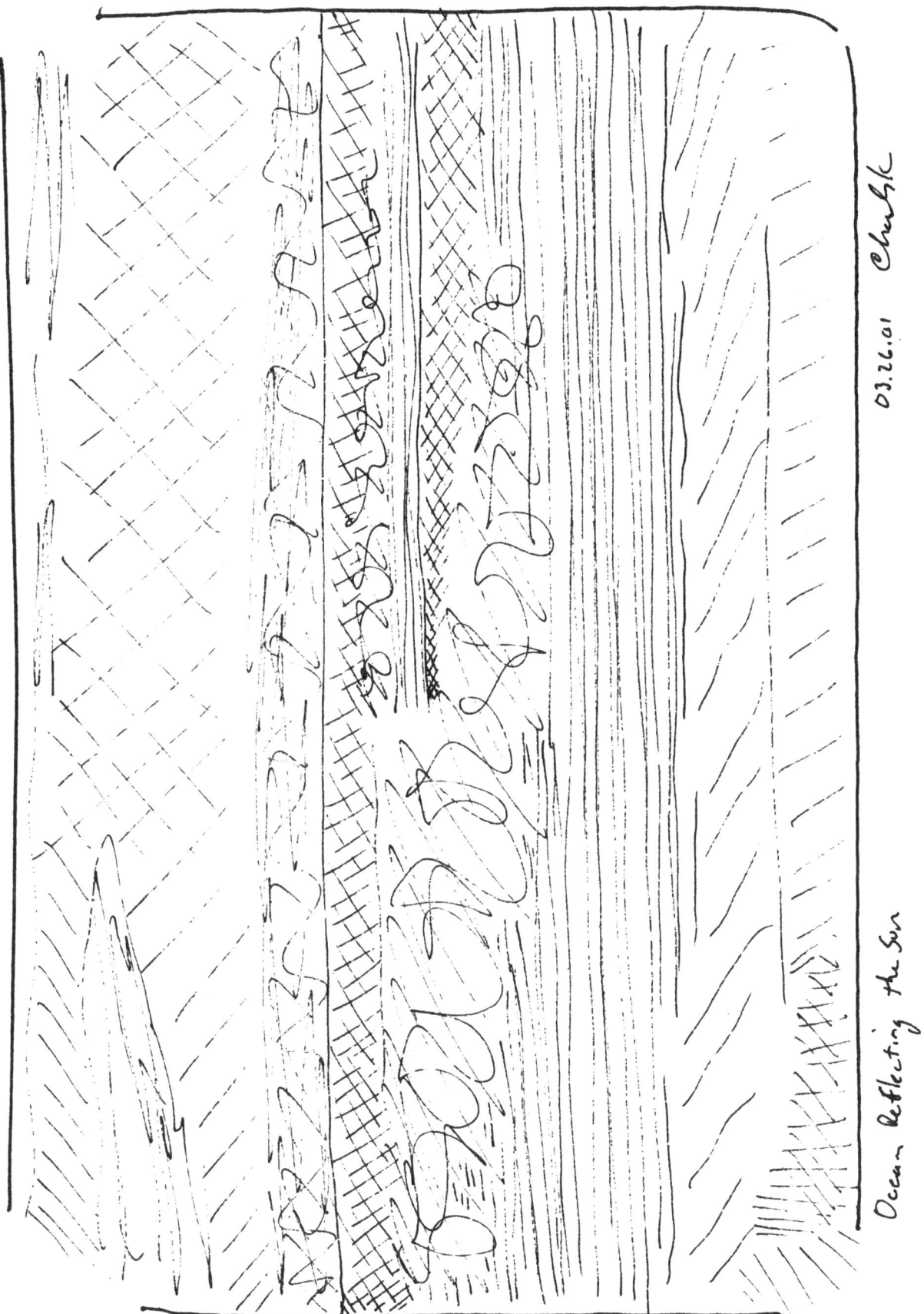

Ocean Reflecting the Sun 03.26.01 @chuck

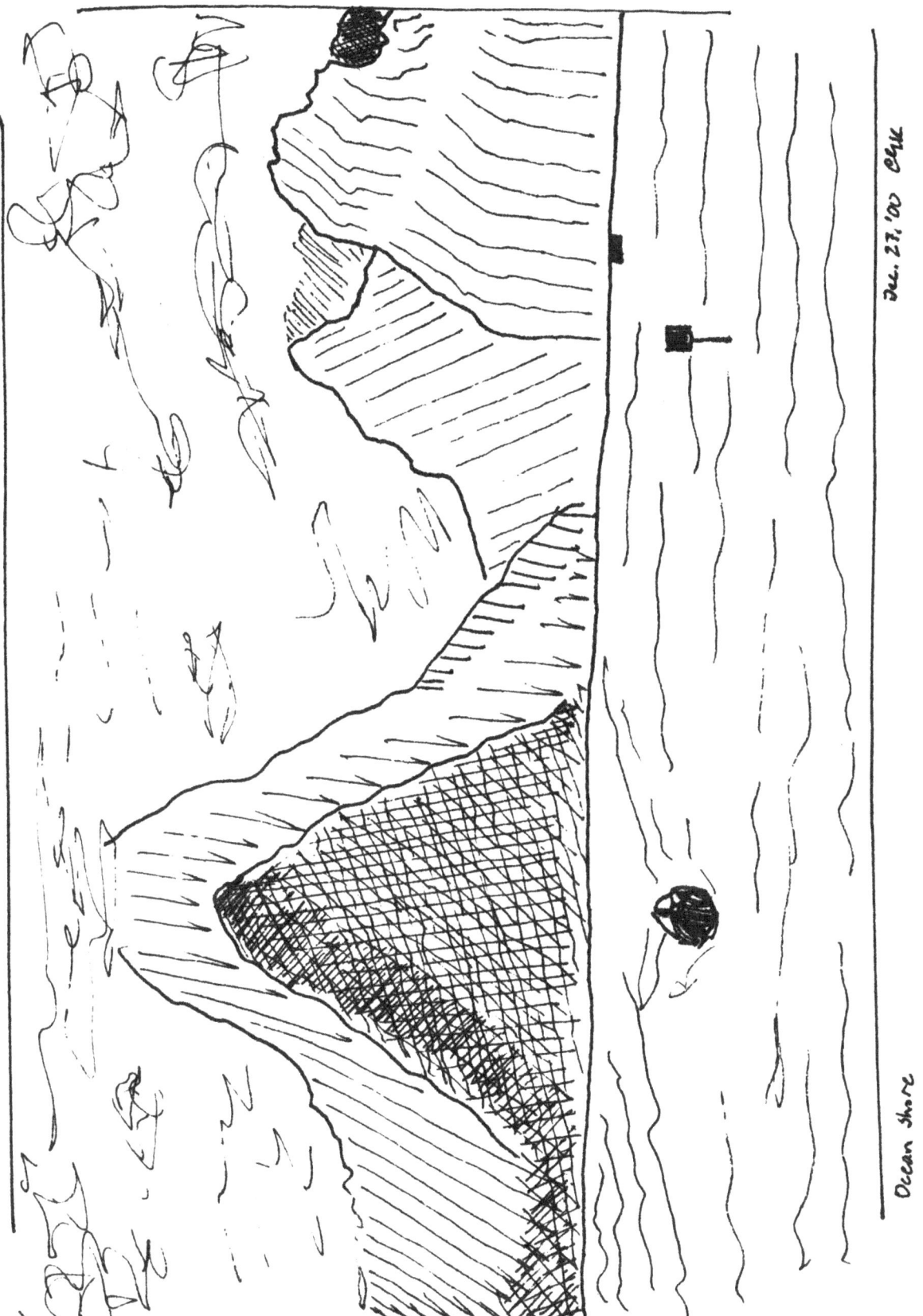

Ocean Shore — Dec. 27, '00 CHK

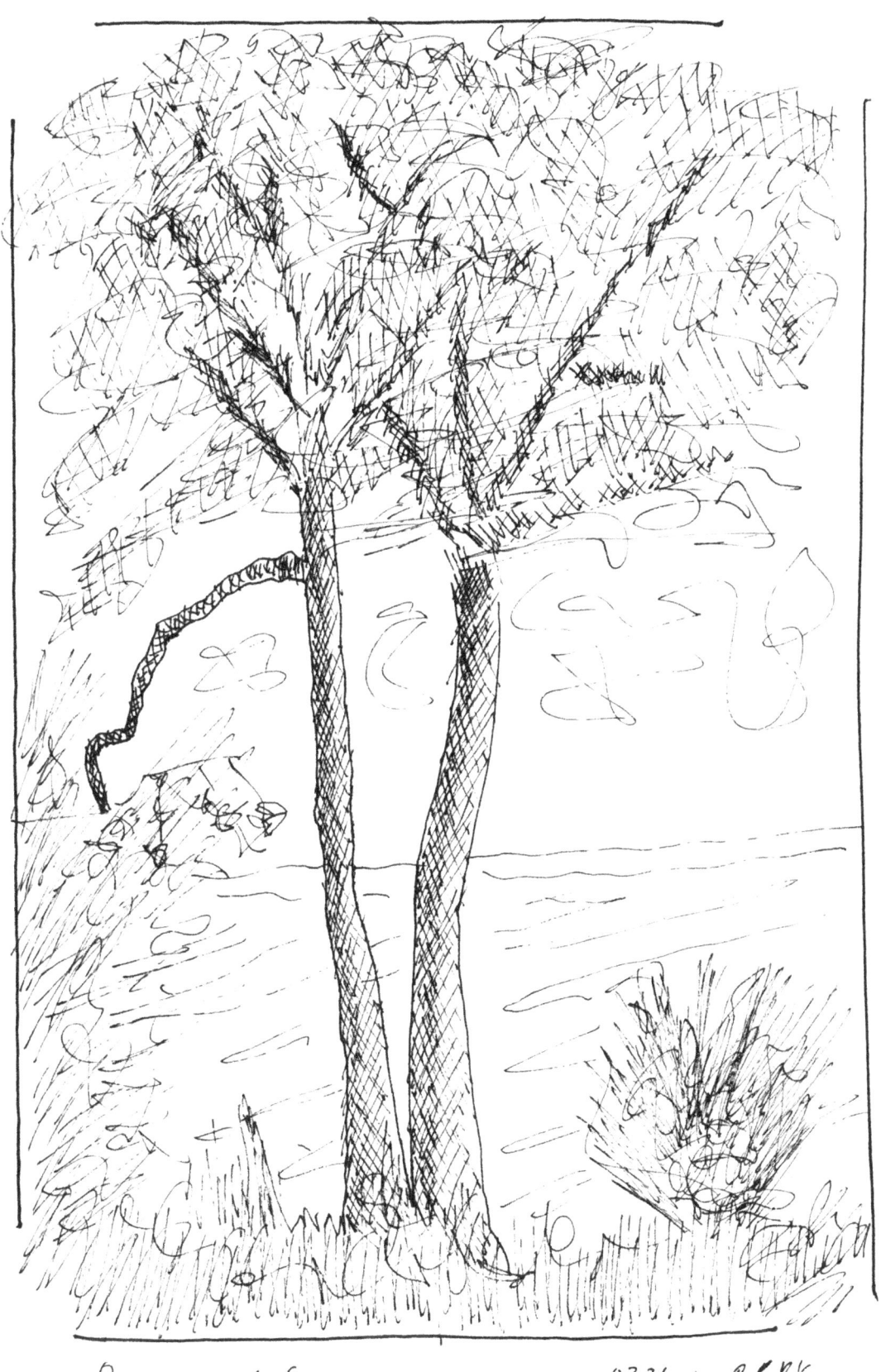

Ocean with Spruce　　　　　03.26.01　C Frank

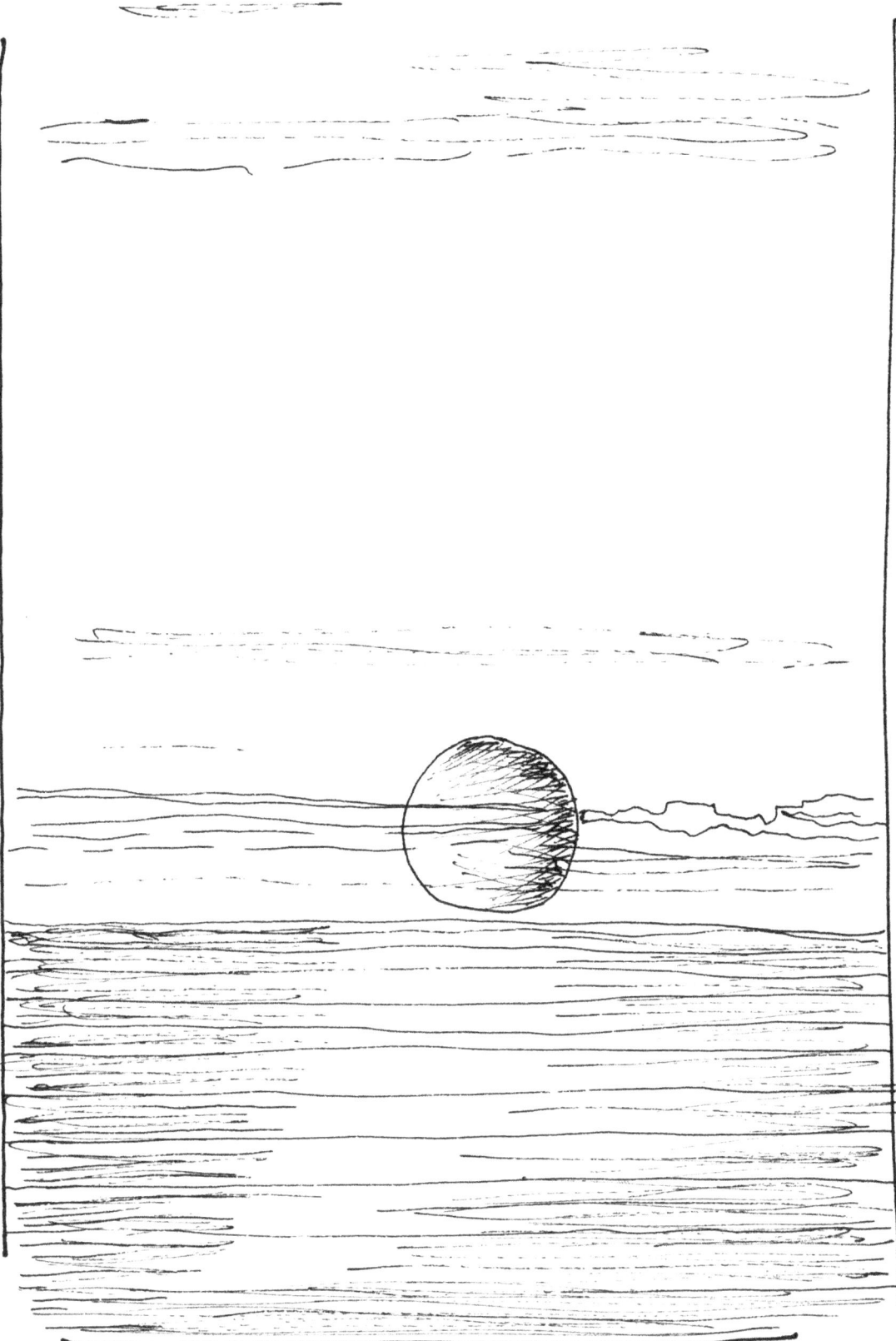

Ocean Sun About to Set   04.02.01   ChuckK

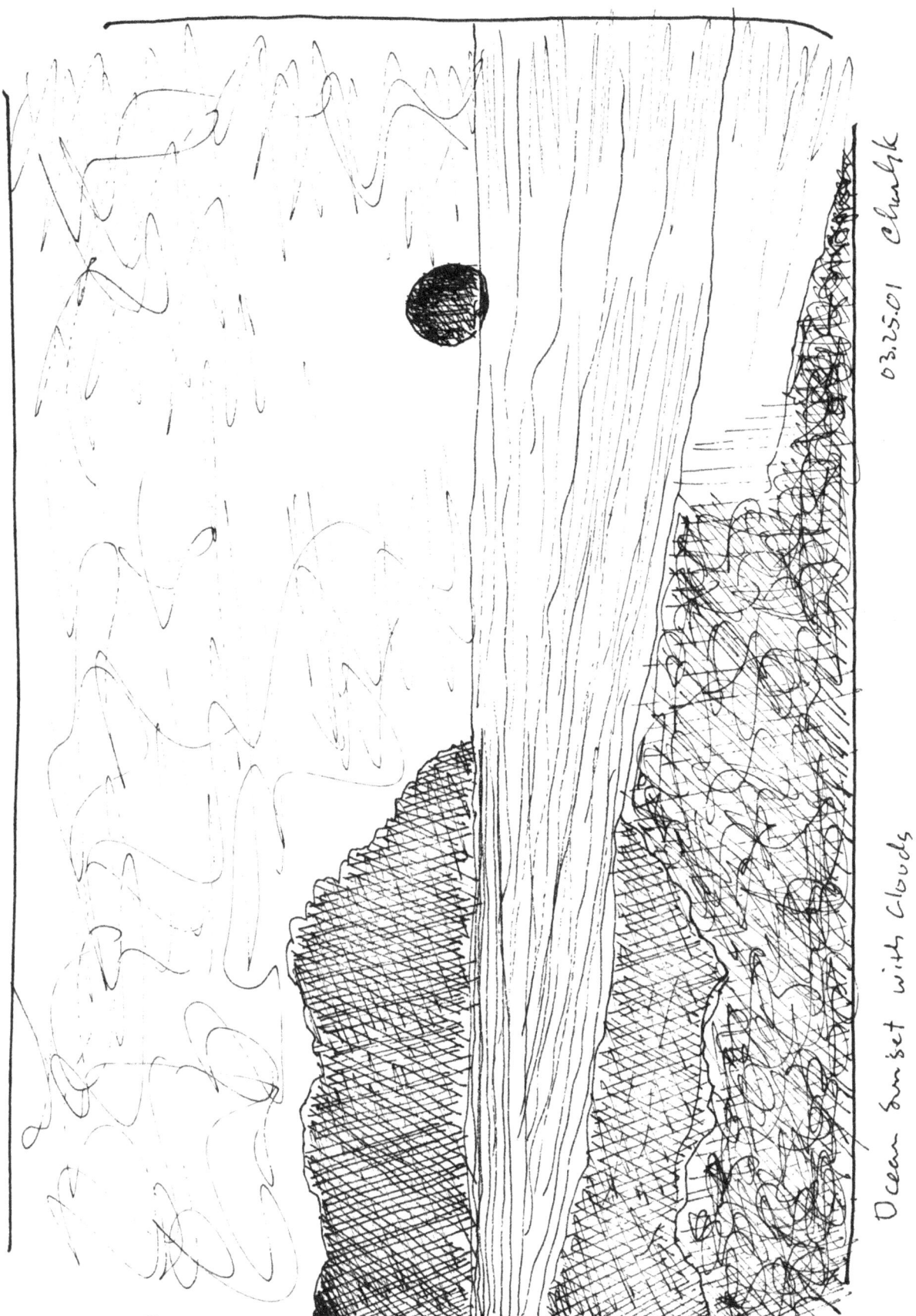

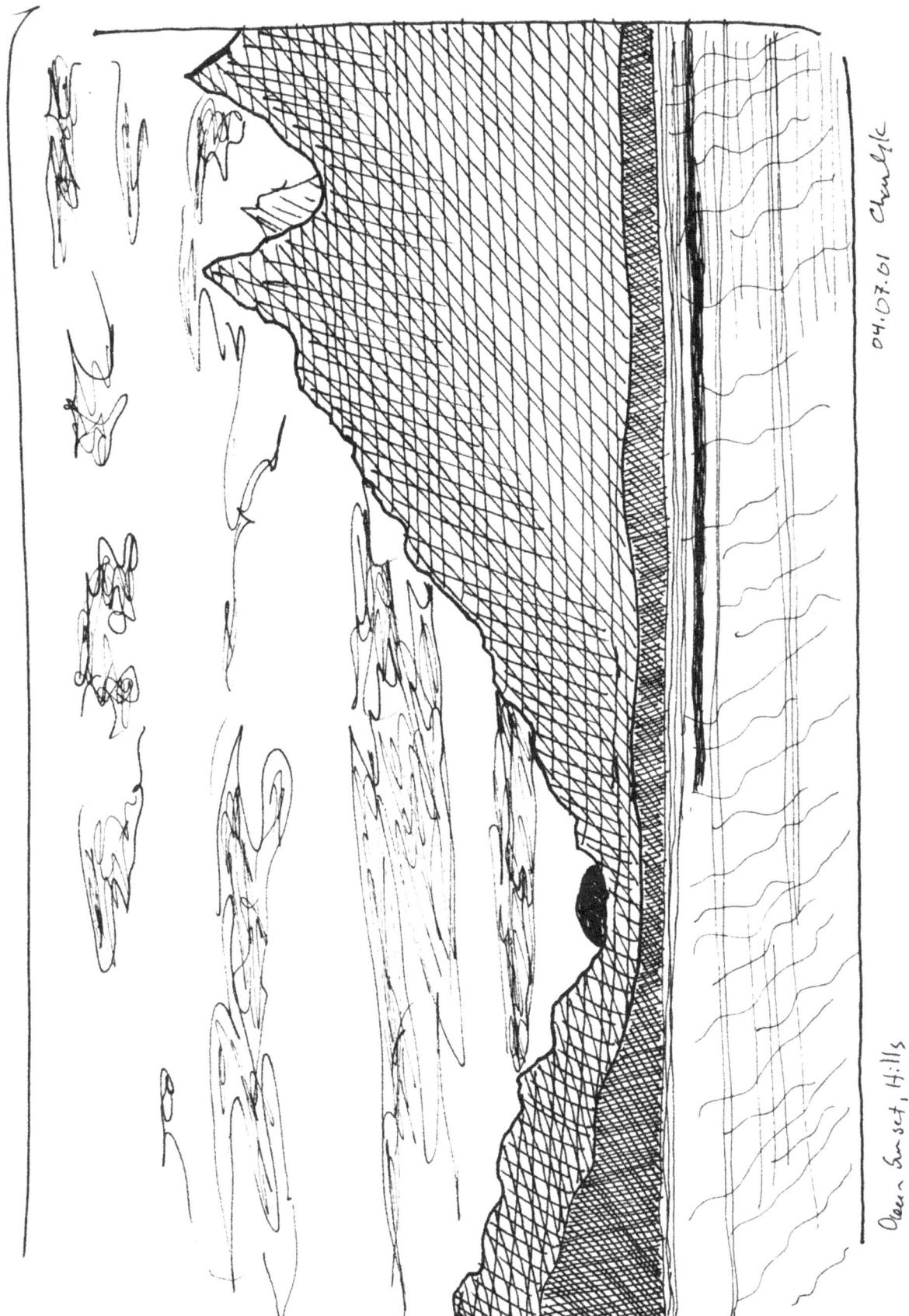

Ocean Sunset, Hills — 04.07.01 Chunlyk

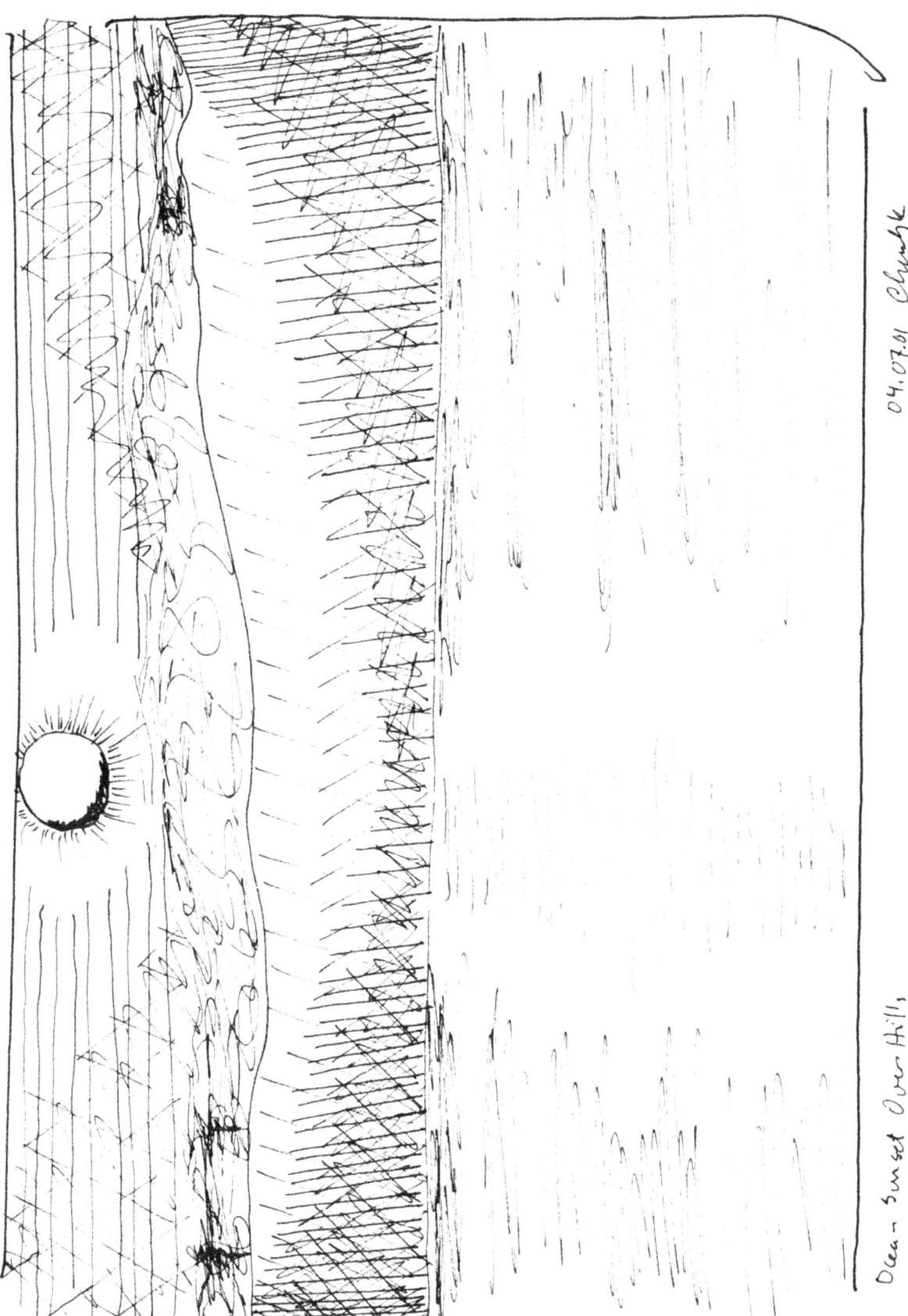

Ocean Sunset Over Hills, 04.07.01 Chudzk

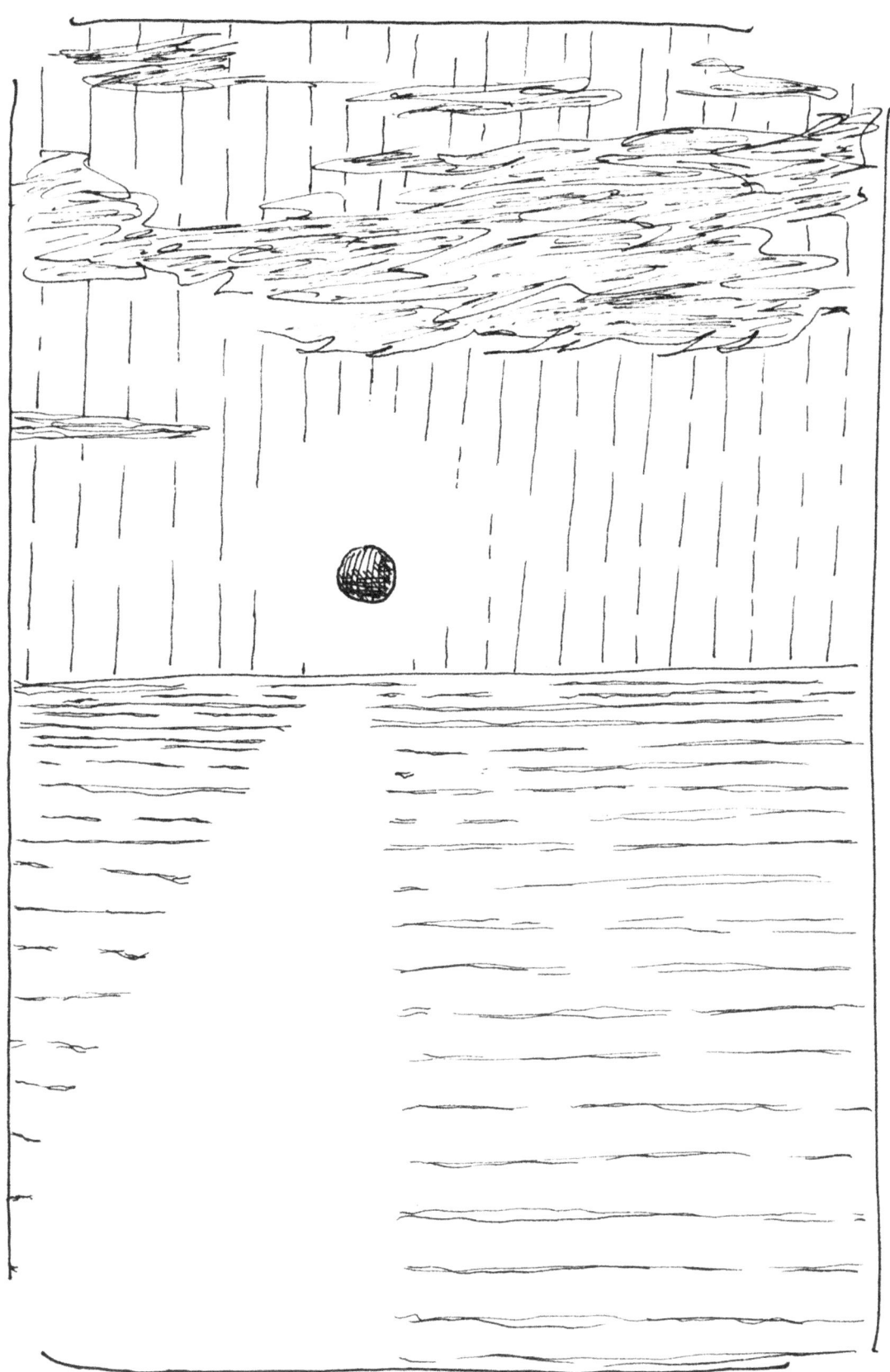

Ocean Sunset Reflecting 04.02.01 Charlie

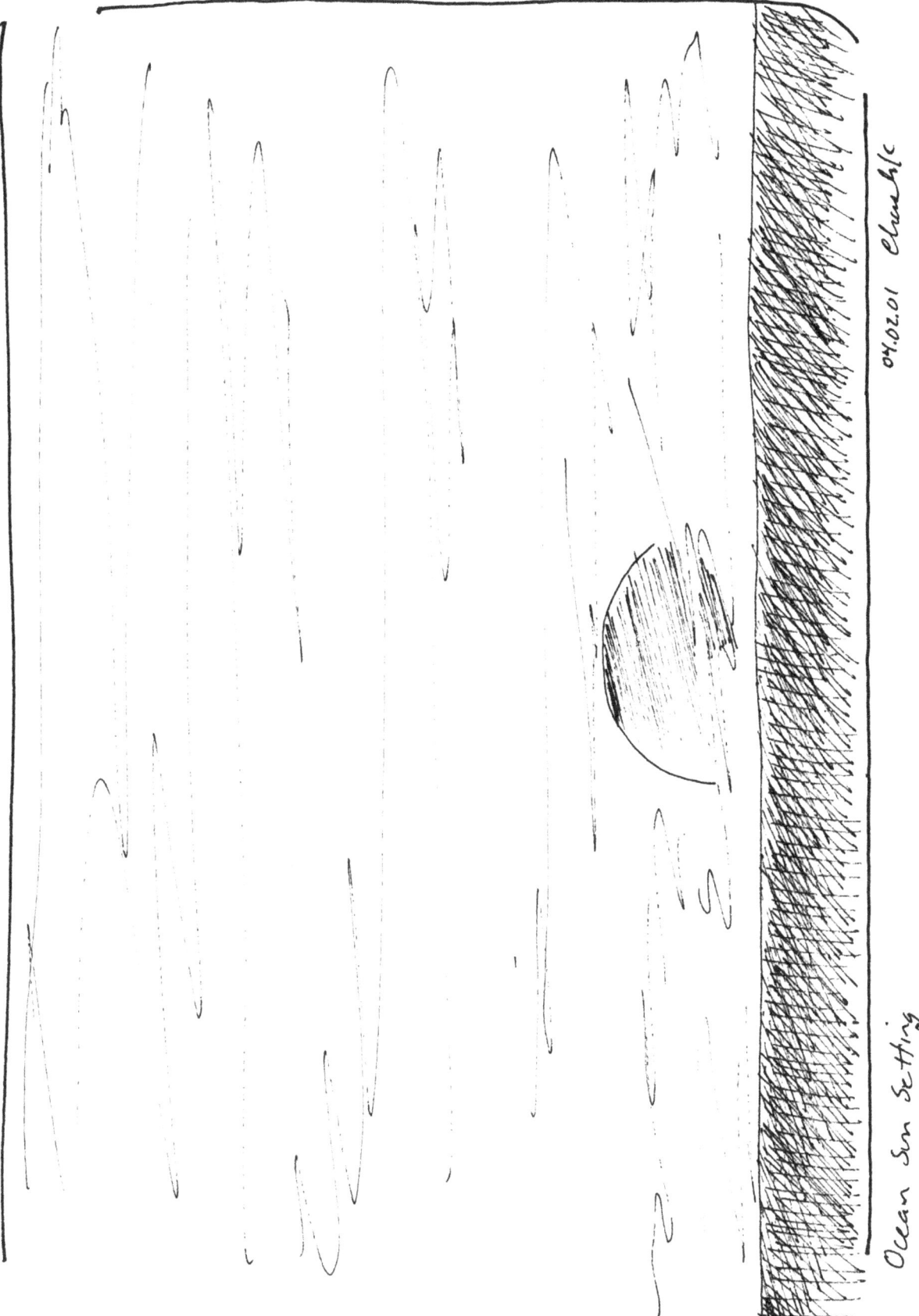

Ocean Sun Setting 04.02.01 chunk/c

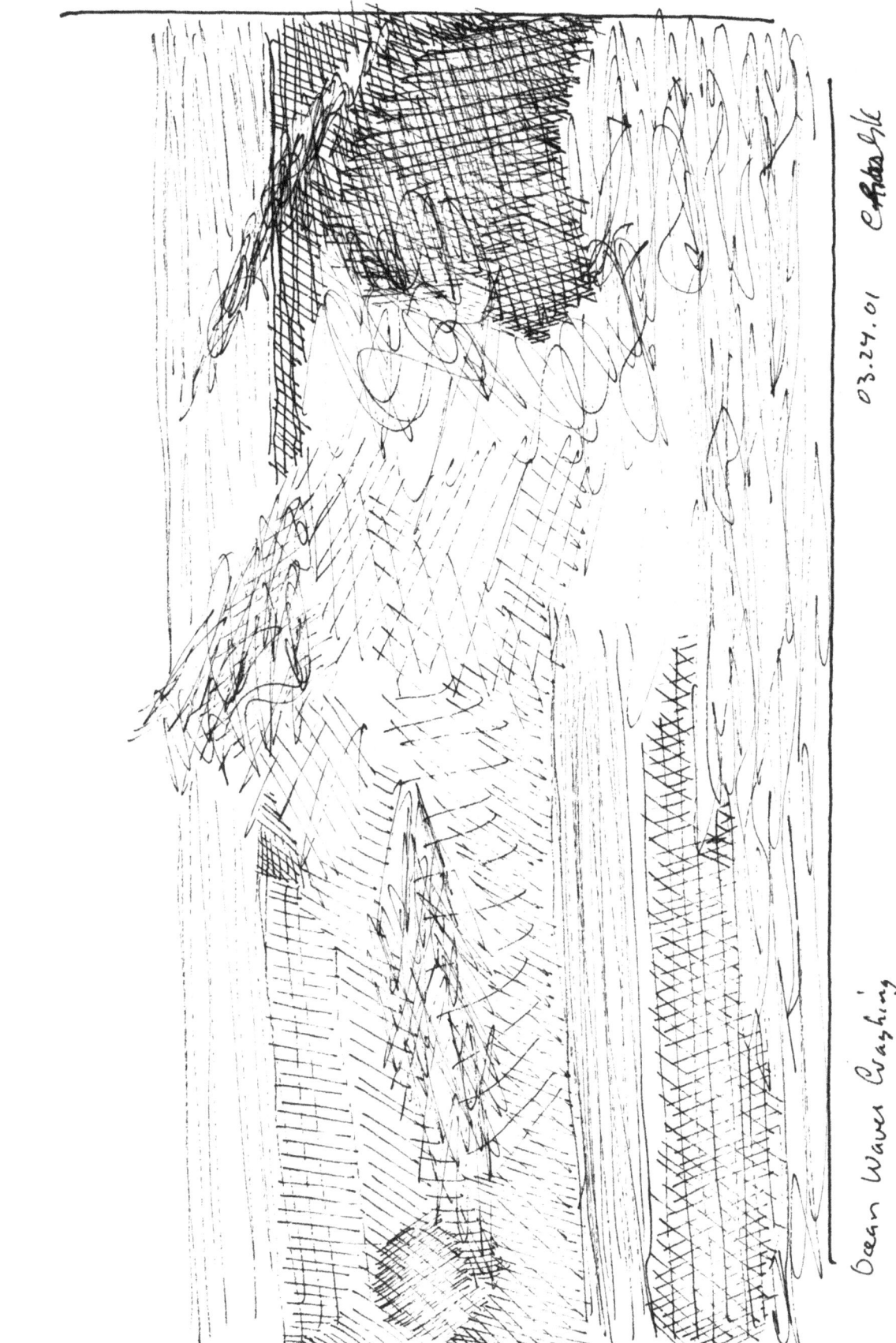
Ocean Waves Crashing — 03.24.01

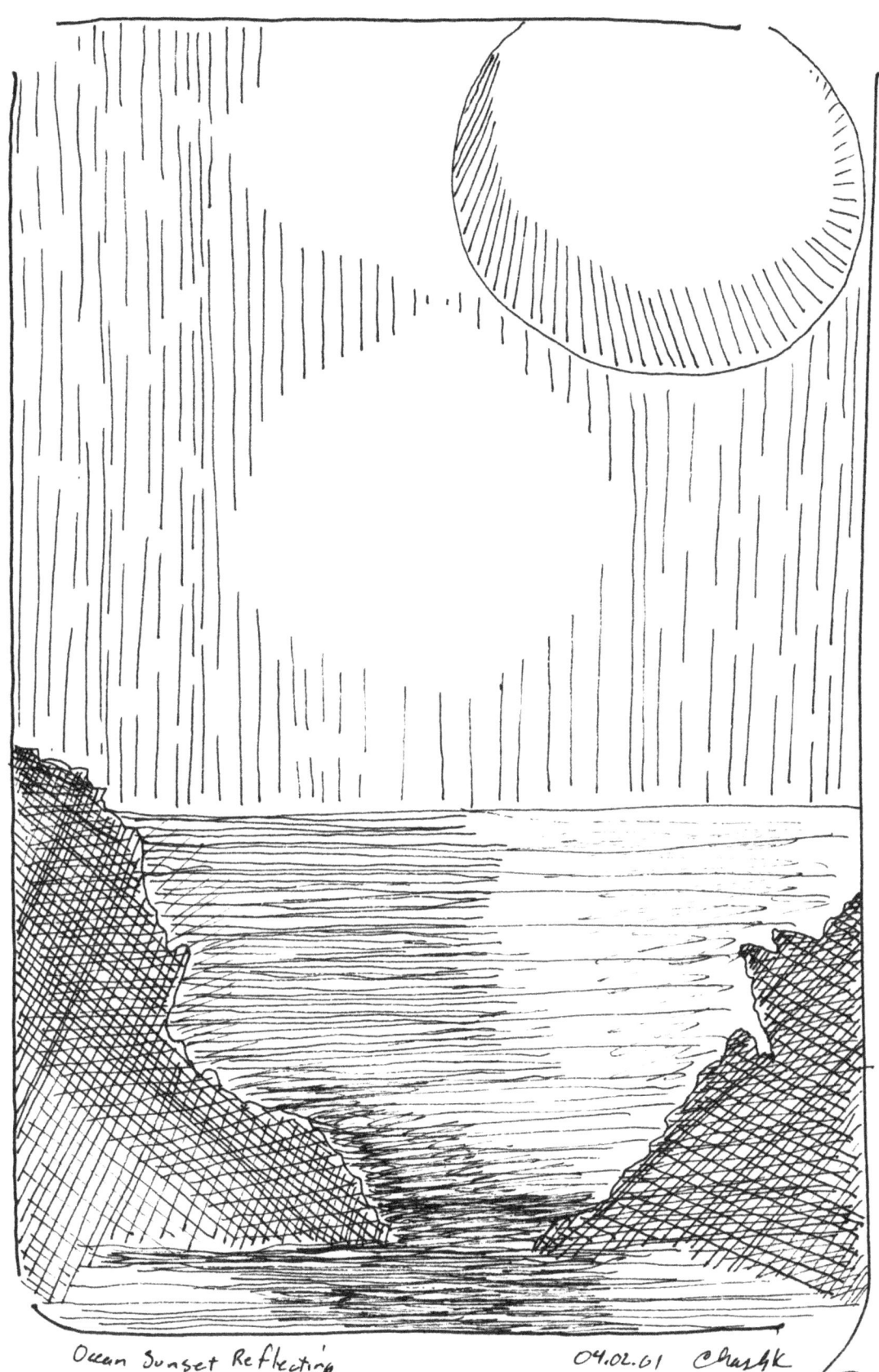

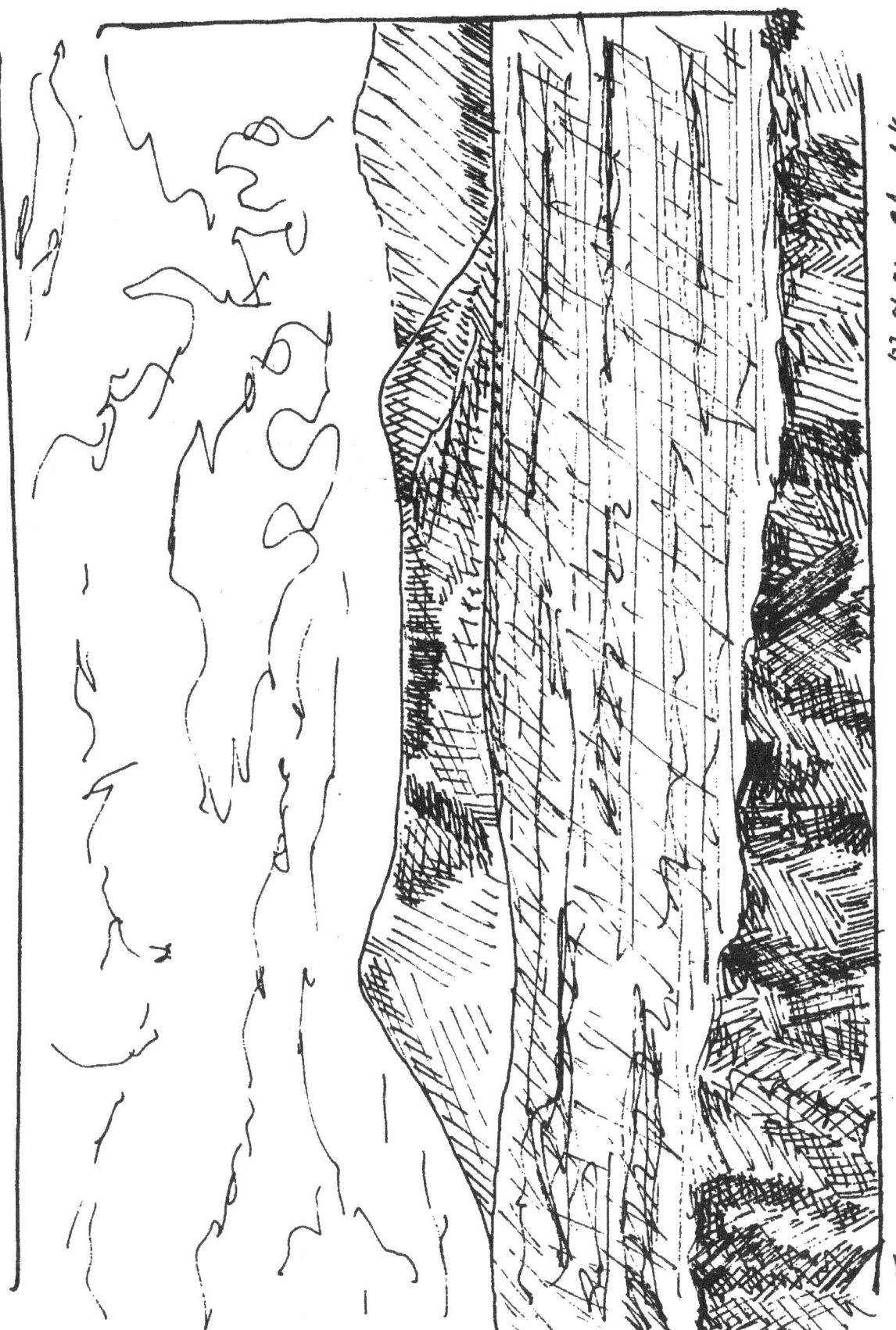

Tanzanian landscape with Clouds — 02.06.01

www.ingramcontent.com/pod-product-compliance
Lightning Source LLC
Chambersburg PA
CBHW082253220526
45469CB00009B/2985